Surgeon Commander Rick Jolly was born in Hong Kong
thirty-seven years ago, and spent his early childhood in
Singapore. He was educated at Stonyhurst and St
Bartholomew's Hospital Medical College in London. After
completing a five year Short-Service Commission as a
Medical Officer in the Royal Navy he resumed postgraduate
studies with the National Health Service in 1979. A year later
he was recalled from the Reserves to command the Royal
Marines Medical Squadron. He was awarded an OBE in 1982
for the tremendous success of his team ashore during the
Falklands campaign.

Married, with one son, his leisure interests include
photography and sub-aqua diving.

'The author has a forthright narrative style ideal for
describing action. With his robust good sense and
determination to get things done, he seems to epitomise the
spirit of the entire Task Force . . . with his eye for detail, his
ebullient patriotism and his nimble pen, the author has
forged a memorable record of his time in the South Atlantic.'
                              Duff Hart-Davis, Sunday Telegraph

'Rich in humour and humanity.'
                              Manchester Evening News

'It is proper that the Ajax Bay story should be told and fortunate that it is related in such a compelling way . . . Apart from vivid accounts of medical repair jobs, the author proves to be a successful raconteur of other aspects of conflict, the grim humour, for instance.'

The Yorkshire Post

'An account of human triumph over the horrors of war . . .'

Coventry Evening Telegraph

'This very honest, forthright and absorbing book will be a further lasting memorial to the men saving life in the midst of battlefield death.'

The Journal, Newcastle-upon-Tyne

'A remarkable record of a remarkable hospital.'

Western Morning News

The Red and Green Life Machine

A Diary of the Falklands Field Hospital

Rick Jolly

Rick Jolly
'88

CORGI BOOKS

THE RED AND GREEN LIFE MACHINE

A CORGI BOOK 0 552 99068 X

Originally published in Great Britain by
Century Publishing Co. Ltd

PRINTING HISTORY

Century edition published 1983
Corgi edition published 1984
Corgi edition reprinted 1984

This book is set in Palatino 10/11½

Corgi Books are published by
Transworld Publishers Ltd.,
Century House, 61–63 Uxbridge Road,
Ealing, London W5 5SA

Printed and bound in Great Britain by
Cox & Wyman Ltd., Reading

For Susie and James

Who, like many other families in the land,
sat and watched the Falklands War unfolding,
and tried not to think about that knock on
the front door.

They also serve ...

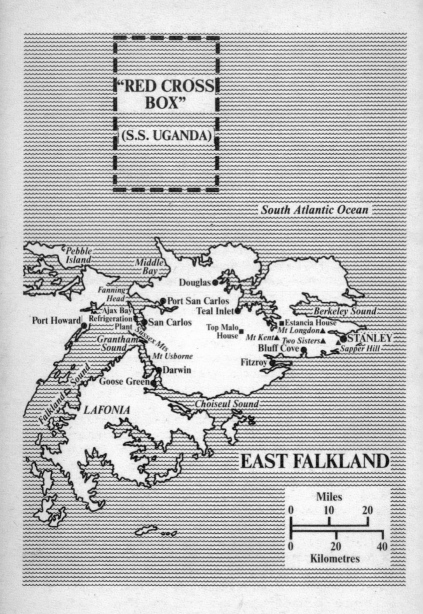

Preface

My desk diary was the last item to be packed as I hurried off to war. This punch-up was going to be different from Belfast, Cyprus, or anything else I'd ever attended, and it seemed to be good planning as well. By making notes at the time events happened, the final report would be that much easier to write.

Well, both diary and I survived, but it was close. The hurried jottings became a priceless personal record. The half-pages for Saturday and Sunday were always overfilled, but then war does not respect the concept of office hours or weekends. The human memory generally declines to store much detail concerning fear or pain, and these details must be written down. Even now I can read the account, then shut my eyes and see that Mirage diving down towards us. But why relive sheer terror? Because it puts other memories into proper perspective, and brings a pleasant glow to them because of the risks that we took. 30,000 men and women went to war in the name of Great Britain to prove a point about civilisation. Freedom is *always* worth fighting for – just ask those who've ever lost it.

I'm grateful to many people for their encouragement and help in expanding an abbreviated record of ten remarkable weeks into something worthy of publication. The photographs come largely from the Commando-trained Nikon of Peter Holgate, but John Williams, Kevin Short, Richard Moody, Frank Gummett and 'Radar' Shields also kindly loaned the results of their photographic skills for publication.

By chance, this is the first book about the Falklands war written by a non-journalist participant. I would therefore like to thank Surgeon Commodore Godfrey Milton-Thompson QHP RN. As the Senior Service's Deputy Medical Director General he read and kindly cleared the text for publication. A large proportion of any royalties will go to Service Charities.

Glossary

(1) ACG	Amphibious Combat Group (Royal Netherlands Marine Korps)
Army/Royal Marines rank (*in ascending order*)	2nd Lieutenant
	Lieutenant
	Captain
	Major
	Lieutenant Colonel
	Colonel
	Brigadier
	Major General
	(Lieutenant General)
Bergan	Rucksack
Bootneck (sl.)	Royal Marines Commando
Buzz (sl.)	Rumour
Cabo	Argentinian Corporal equivalent
CAP	Combat Air Patrol
Chacon	Wooden or metal freight container
CINCFLEET	Commander-in-Chief, Fleet (Northwood)
CO	Commanding Officer
Compo rations	Composite rations (concentrated food)
CP	Command Post
Cpl	Corporal
CPOMA	Chief Petty Officer Medical Assistant
Div.	Division
FCMA	Fleet Chief Medical Assistant
Flyco	Flight Control (on aviation-capable ship)
FRO	Field Record Office
Fuerza Aerea Argentina	Argentinian Air Force

GPMG	General Purpose Machine Gun
LCU	Landing Craft Utility
LFFI	Land Forces Falklands Islands
LMA	Leading Medical Assistant
LPD	Landing Platform Dock (HMS *Intrepid, Fearless*)
LPH	Landing Platform Helicopter (HMS *Hermes*)
LS	Landing Site
LSL	Landing Ship Logistic
MA	Medical Assistant
Middle Wallop	Headquarters and main base of Army Air Corps, Hampshire
Milan	Anti-tank missile
MO	Medical Officer
MOIC	Medical Officer In Charge
Mushroom	Radio call-sign of logistics officer
NATO	North Atlantic Treaty Organisation
Naval rank	
(*in ascending order*)	Sub Lieutenant
	Lieutenant (Lt)
	Lieutenant Commander (Lt Cdr)
	Commander (Cdr)
	Captain
	Commodore
	Rear Admiral
	Vice Admiral
	Admiral
	(Medical Officers' rank is similar, but with prefix 'Surgeon')
O Group	Orders Group (meeting attended by key unit personnel)
OP	Observation Post
PCT	Parachute Clearing Troop
PMO	Principal Medical Officer
POMA	Petty Officer Medical Assistant
PT	Physical Training
PW/POW	Prisoner (of) War
RAF	Royal Air Force
RAMC	Royal Army Medical Corps

RAP	Regimental Aid Post
RCB	Red Cross Box
REME	Royal Electrical and Mechanical Engineers
RFA	Royal Fleet Auxiliary
'Royal' (sl.)	Royal Marines Commando
RSM	Regimental Sergeant Major
sangar	Built-up defensive position
SAS	Special Air Service (Regiment)
Satcom	Satellite Communications (Terminal)
SBS	Special Boat Squadron (Royal Marines)
SLR	Self-loading Rifle
SNEB	50mm unguided rocket projectile (of French manufacture)
SST	Surgical Support Team
Starlight	Radio call-sign of medical officer
TEZ	Total Exclusion Zone
'Toms' (sl.)	Private soldier in (especially) Parachute Regiment
triage	Sorting of medical priorities
UXB	Unexploded Bomb
WO1	Warrant Officer, First Class
WO2	Warrant Officer, Second Class

Friday, May 21

As I swing back in to check the bearing, Corporal Gleeson points upwards past my shoulder. From the north, accelerating as they dive, four Mirages begin an attack on HMS *Antrim*. Like a mother tiger prowling restlessly in the neck of San Carlos Water as she protects her cubs behind, the big guided missile destroyer spits back her defiance. The line of splashes caused by Mirage cannon shells now meets her tall, grey flanks and for several seconds she absorbs hundreds of direct hits.

The fourth Mirage has other ideas. Disturbed by the rising cloud of red tracer, he breaks off left and straightens up, heading directly for us. Corporal Gleeson cocks the GPMG and begins to fire upwards at the lethal outline that we now see expanding rapidly. Are the leading edges of the Mirage twinkling with cannon fire? My decision is reflex. Jumping down, I dive straight into the ditch. Better a clean death here from a 30mm shell through the head than incineration and fragmentation in a whirling maelstrom of ruptured fuel tanks and broken rotor blades . . .

In early March 1982 it would have been very hard to imagine that, ten weeks later, we would be at war. The annual NATO winter exercises in Arctic Norway were about to begin, and the South Atlantic was over 8,000 miles away . . .

March 5 – 16 1982

The Defence cuts announced in 1981 have begun to bite, in a small way as far as overall spending is concerned, but in a big way for the Royal Marines. This year our involvement in the normal winter training in Norway has been much reduced. 45 Commando RM, just back from a four-month tour in Northern Ireland, are not even deploying to refresh their considerable Arctic warfare skills.

For me, too, there is no opportunity to consolidate the friendships made last winter with the doctors at the Trondheim Central Sykehuset – the main hospital of that lovely city. Instead, Lieutenant Fred Cook, my second in command, has gone to Norway in charge of a scaled-down version of Medical Squadron. Some are new to the dark and painful secrets of cross-country skiing with a 30kg rucksack on the back. They will learn, as I had to, that a loaded 'bergan' needs little encouragement to take charge of a wobbling skier going downhill. The still mountain air will echo with their shouts and yells, as well as the roars of laughter from more accomplished comrades as the novices fall over. Sometimes the arrest of forward motion is horrendously painful – the 'tree-stop' technique; on other occasions skier, skis and bergan explode the deep drifts into a welter of shining white snow particles, a procedure known in the Corps as 'doing a yeti'.

During my Arctic warfare training in 1981 I 'yettied' so often and so spectacularly that the other Royal Marines in my group awarded me a special end-of-course prize. With the lovely humour for which the Corps is justly famous, they gave me the accolade of 'the Jacques Cousteau of downhill skiing'!

This year will be different, I have had to stay behind and hold the fort, while Fred and his training team are ensuring that Medical Squadron novices reach the standard required. Their final exercise will feature four nights out without resupply, and 40 kilometres of tactical cross-country skiing culminating in a dawn attack across a frozen river. There have been compensations, however, including a weekend trip to the Danish Army Medical School outside Copenhagen, where I have been asked to talk about my medical experiences in Northern Ireland, with particular reference to the injuries of urban guerrilla warfare. The Reservist Medical Officers are a keen, well-motivated bunch of civilians who seem to love their country and who plan seriously for war. They cannot understand the reasons for this particular conflict in Britain's backyard, but my colour slides of gunshot wounds and blast injuries certainly come as a shock to some of the audience. They quickly get over their disturbed feelings when I stress that this is a normal phenomenon. Their questions are shrewd, the hospitality traditional.

Now we are flying north to Evenes airfield, hundreds of miles inside the Arctic Circle. A team of officers from 3rd Commando Brigade Headquarters have been appointed umpires in their appropriate skills for the traditional final exercise codenamed 'Alloy Express '82'. For once I am going to be able to see how the other NATO nations run their casualty evacuation and medical support systems. It will be a huge exercise with several thousand American, Dutch and Royal Marines ranged against the Norwegians, as well as British, Canadian, Italian and German infantry and logistic units.

First, we are to prepare ourselves for life in the field again. A motel at Sjovegan provides wonderful comfort, while the well-lit community ski-track and the frozen fjord alongside the small town provide the means for necessary exercise and we are soon match-fit again. The Norwegian children giggle at our broad wooden skis, more rudely known throughout the Corps as 'pussers' planks'. Despite the heavy metal bindings they are strong, cheap, reliable and regarded with some affection.

Our chief umpire is Brigadier Julian Thompson RM, a small, dark, wiry man with a cheerful smile and a mind like a carbon steel scalpel. For his age he is ridiculously fit. As a young officer he also trained as a parachutist and commanded a reconnaissance troop, so he understands perfectly the

15

practical problems of this harsh climate and terrain. He is also as capable as any young Marine in his exploitation of ground and cover, both personally and as part of a Strategic Force plan. Along with many others, I admire his qualities immensely. Here is a leader we will cheerfully follow into battle, confident that he will acquire the necessary information and make the correct decisions. Typically, he is frustrated at not playing an active part in the exercise; back in Plymouth, some months before, he had personally decided to allow 42 Commando RM and 1 ACG to come under American command. Now his sharp eye and endless energy are devoted to assessing and recording. The poacher is taking a short sabbatical as gamekeeper.

While we wait for the amphibious landings to commence, and finalize our umpiring tasks from the numerous and endless briefings at Exercise HQ in Bardufoss, I get to know my room-mate well. Major Nigel Willoughby has just completed a massive and important study on the future medical resources needed for Commando Forces at war. We have much to discuss, and burn the midnight oil drinking our duty-free malt whisky on several occasions. He was the Officer Commanding Naval Party 8901, the Royal Marines detachment in the Falklands Islands, in 1977. During his tour of duty there one of the two Government Beaver floatplane pilots was badly injured in a crash, and the other fell ill so, as a qualified Army pilot, he took up flying again.

His description of the rugged terrain, the beautifully clean air and incredibly rich wildlife, the friendliness of the population and their gratitude for his efforts, make me sad that I shall never have an opportunity to visit the Islands. Although the ship carries a Medical Officer, the Ministry of Defence has decided to retire HMS *Endurance* from active service at the end of 1982. The nearest I shall now get to the Falklands will be the pictures taken during this last commission by my friend and neighbour, Lieutenant Commander Andrew Lockett, the ships' Meteorological Officer.

The exercise finally gets under way and starts badly, because the US Marine Corps' giant Amtrak amphibious personnel carriers remain confined on board the landing ships. A fierce 50-knot wind whips up the placid waters of

Andoyfjord into a steep chop which would swamp the lumbering beasts. From the next fjord along, 42 Commando and 1 ACG somehow (and rather embarrassingly) get ashore, thanks to brillant flying by their Fleet Air Arm support helicopters. For 24 hours they sit awaiting orders, until eventually the 36th Marine Assault Unit 'hits the beach' under the eyes of some curious Norwegian spectators.

The war is behind schedule and there is a lot of catching up to be done. A succession of clear blue skies helps the script unfold but, although pleasant, the weather is no real test for anyone. Noisy gaggles of Huey and Sea Stallion helicopters float through the crisp mountain air in huge *Apocalypse Now* formations, their pilots unable to shake Vietnam and total air superiority from their training or concept of operations. The GR3 Harriers of 1(F) Squadron RAF have a field day with their camera guns, as they swoop down from the sun and make repeated passes, working over the flocks of helicopters like mountain dogs cutting out sheep.

On the southern flank 42 Commando seem to be enjoying things after the initial confusion. It is my old unit so I've a special affection for them. Unusually there are two Medical Officers for this year's deployment, providing a sensible overlap during which the newcomer can undergo his Arctic warfare training. In the back of the RAP Volvo bandwagon I spend quite a lot of time chatting to them both.

Ross Adley, a Barts man like me, is soon off to Peru on the Joint Services Hovercraft Expedition – a splendid bit of swanning before he starts his hospital training in anaesthetics. For Crispin Swinhoe, his successor, congratulations are also in order because he has completed the parachute training course and can now wear para wings on his pyjamas if he likes. They are an amusing pair and good company.

Not far away, the three rifle companies are dug in to a series of carefully chosen positions that cover road junctions, bridges and some helicopter landing sites. 42 Commando's companies are always lettered K, L, and M: Kilo, Lima and Mike. However, the Marines have their own phonetic label – Kiss, Lick and Munch. The 'Mighty Munch' is commanded by Captain Chris Nunn; he is another old friend as well as my son's godfather.

But there are other things to see and report on. The Norwegians have an inflatable field dressing station of ultra-modern design which I much admire and take many pictures of. In the logistic support area behind the airfield at Bardu, a German Army field hospital has been set up. Teutonic efficiency abounds in its design and construction. Interlocking wooden pallets act as duckboards to keep feet clear of the frozen ground. Tacked on at one end of the tented complex is a small building which looks like a caravan on lifting jacks, and inside this structure is a really bright and modern operating theatre.

A Bulldog (non-exercise) casualty arrives in a Royal Air Force Pump helicopter whose spinning rotors create a mini-blizzard on the edge of the landing site. The young British soldier it carries has fallen off a Scorpion armoured vehicle and has hit his head. Semi-conscious, he is carefully examined by the hospital's neurologist who also inspects a technically perfect set of skull X-rays a few minutes later. All is well, and the umpire is favourably impressed.

The possession of a neutral vehicle enables an umpire to go anywhere he likes, so I look at the 'enemy' too. The US Marine Corps Logistic Support Battalion have tried to dig into the frozen training areas just outside Elvagardsmoen Camp. A fierce wind sweeps down the valley on to the four linked shipping containers that make up the medical complex, but inside, the staff and patients are warm and comfortable. Their comfort may be short-lived however, since warm objects tend to sink slowly into frozen ice and snow.

Forty miles farther along the twisting roads, but a quarter of that distance by helicopter, my own Medical Squadron have set up shop in a hall overlooking a small seafaring village. The boys seem happy, although their limited numbers make serious medical exercise casualty play impossible. Instead, they are manning a Bulldog sick bay, an accommodation and assessment facility for the inevitable minor but genuine injuries and illnesses that will occur. A small team called a Collecting Section has deployed forward with 42 Commando, while 1 ACG have also sent some staff and an ambulance to help with the Bulldog work.

Keeping up standards, we also invite No. 3 Troop's boss,

Lieutenant Malcolm Higgins RN, to dinner. He is leaving the Regiment for an appointment to the Royal Naval Hospital at Haslar, near Portsmouth. Bow ties are *de rigueur*, made from cardboard and black masking tape, while in the galley our chefs work miracles with tinned compo rations, supplemented by a little locally purchased fresh. The Commanding Officer of the Regiment, Lieutenant Colonel Ivar Hellberg, is also present, and he and I donate a couple of bottles of wine each to help proceedings along. It is a very pleasant way to be 'dined out' of the Regiment, although we will seek to repeat the occasion more formally when we get back to Plymouth.

Eventually the exercise comes to its predetermined ending both in the correct place and at the right time. After a lengthy wait at Bardufoss Airfield we scramble gratefully into a laden Hercules for the six-hour bash home. Cottonwool plugs, ear defenders and cold weather caps are worn in varying combinations to ensure some kind of fitful doze as the aircraft drones and vibrates through the bumpy air, and the minutes tick by reluctantly. Ahead lies Easter leave and a spell at home in our Plymouth base, before the summer exercises on Salisbury Plain begin. It is all a pleasant prospect as I drift into sleep at last.

Friday, April 2

Incredibly, it wasn't an April Fool's Day joke after all. The Argentinians *have* done it. At 0230 this morning the Cabinet were told in London that an invasion force had landed and taken over Port Stanley, the capital of the Falkland Islands. The Royal Marines of Naval Party 8901 put up a stiff fight but eventually succumbed to sheer weight of numbers. I hope casualties have been light, but throughout the Corps there is quiet anger and a determination to redress the grievance of defeat.

At some unholy hour, Ivar Hellberg is called to the Mount Wise Headquarters of Commando Forces RM. He is told that a Task Force is being prepared to sail with all despatch to the South Atlantic, and that, like all the other units of 3rd Commando Brigade, the Commando Logistic Regiment's Easter leave is cancelled. He must now make plans to collect and deliver several thousand tons of War Maintenance Reserve stores to the various ports, a tremendous effort which must be completed in 72 hours instead of the more normal planning targets.

The CO is grim-faced as he summons us for an O (Orders) Group. It is going to be very difficult to meet his target, particularly as British Rail are unable to help. Not only is it the weekend, but the rolling stock has not been pre-positioned as it would have been in time of tension. It seems that the Argentinian sequestration has caught everyone, including the Foreign and Commonwealth Office, on the hop. Transport Squadron begin the long grind up the motorway to the ammunition depots around the country, a major effort that will see them completing the equivalent mileage of *five* times to the Falklands and back before we sail.

For me there are a few other buttons to push. The Defence Medical Equipment Depot in Hampshire has already been alerted, and is packing and despatching Naval medical war stores for the Fleet as fast as it can. My request for the Royal Marines' medical supplements is met with a cheerful 'can-do' attitude, by Captain Chas Kirton, the Mobilisation Stores Officer at the Depot. By first light on Saturday we have all the surgical stores for our two Naval Surgical Support Teams down in Coypool. The teams themselves are also mobilized, one from the Royal Naval Hospital Plymouth and the other from RNH Haslar. The Haslar team also arrive that night, handicapped by the absence of their Administrative Officer who is on leave, abroad. There is also another problem. Because we are likely to deploy to war in RN ships, a Command decision is taken – no women in the surgical teams. This removes the female nursing element at a stroke, and gives the SST leaders great problems in finding suitable male replacements in time. Needless to say, the girls are a bit upset about the whole thing too.

Events move swiftly. The Senior Medical Officer at HQ Commando Forces, Surgeon Captain Barry Blackstone, is also away so I call into the HQ at regular intervals to give advice as well as seek information. The senior officer in charge of logistics and personnel, Colonel Ian Baxter, takes me aside early on Saturday. The Ministry of Defence are requisitioning the luxury liner *Canberra*, now on the last leg of a round-the-world voyage. She is due in Southampton on the following Wednesday, but meanwhile I am to be one of a small advance party that will leave tomorrow for Gibraltar, and join the ship there.

More frantic preparations as I put the reins once more in Fred Cook's capable hands. There is just time for a last brief to the two Surgical Support Teams. The stores are being transferred into wooden logistic containers named 'chacons'. As there are no roads worth speaking about in the Falklands, it will not make sense to take the vehicles which normally carry all our stores. We realise that Her Majesty's Government is being rather serious about the whole endeavour when we ask for over 30 chacons to be delivered. Normally the delay between ordering and receiving can be measured in months. Now, a stream of dockyard lorries produces that number the following day.

There is also opportunity for a quick discussion with the

Deputy Medical Director General of the Royal Navy, Surgeon Commodore Godfrey Milton-Thompson. He is down in Plymouth as a guest of the Medical Officer in Charge of Stonehouse, Surgeon Captain Jim Cox. They are both helpful and generous in allowing me to take Surgeon Commander George Rudge, a maxillo-facial and jaw surgeon as part of the team. George is immaculate in white tie and tails as front-of-house manager of the splendid Officers' Mess revue, *April Frolich's*. The title is a pun on an obscure medical disorder. He's delighted with the news. One of the performers is a consultant physician, Surgeon Commander John Williams, who enviously wishes us luck, little realizing that he too will be mobilized within hours and sent to join *Canberra*.

Sunday, April 4

My family rise and breakfast early, as we have 100 miles to cover before 0930, my reporting time for the Gibraltar flight. The journey up to Somerset is uneventful, apart from the stream of lorries heading the other way to Plymouth. Some are recognizable by their battleplate numbers as Transport Squadron vehicles; most are down on their axles and moving slowly with heavy loads of artillery ammunition.

Despite all the secrecy that supposedly surrounds our departure, Yeovilton Naval Air Station is throbbing and the main car park by the Museum full of interested spectators. Parked near them on the apron, a four-engined Belfast freighter is ingesting two stripped-down Wessex helicopters into its massive belly. I visit a Fleet Air Arm chum in Station Flight for a chat, then hear the familiar whine of Sea Harrier engines. A flight of four aircraft taxis past and line up for take-off. James, my nine-year-old son, thinks they have laid on the whole performance just for him and we wave as the quartet rolls forward in a noisy stream take-off. Then it is my turn. As the Hercules trundles sedately down to the end of the duty runway, I catch a glimpse of Susie and James standing by the car. It is no use waving back. I am off to war and this may be my last sight of them. Minutes later we are accelerating down the broad asphalt ribbon, then climbing steeply above the patchwork fields of England before setting course for the south.

The crew are very friendly and invite us up to the flight deck where we chat. Leading the party is Captain Robert Ward, a Royal Marines officer who is a free-fall parachuting enthusiast. Our *Canberra* liaison officer is Sammy Bradford, a Deputy Captain who knows the ship intimately, having actually commanded her. He is also a Captain in the Royal Navy Reserve and therefore understands the needs of the Senior Service.

Our aircraft is eventually heading for Ascension Island, a pimple of volcanic ash just below the Equator. Its hold is loaded with engineering spares and crew for the two Wessex helicopters following us in the Belfast. Four hours later we let down through cloud, well clear of the Pillars of Hercules, then turn in towards the Rock. Our cold, dry aircraft is now scudding along over a grey Atlantic, through warm moist air. The tricky turn on to finals along the edge of Spanish airspace demands intense concentration. I watch, fascinated, as several large drops of condensed moisture fall from the overhead panels straight down the pilot's neck. Suddenly the co-pilot increases power and we overshoot the tiny runway, climb and then trundle around the Rock again. A nosewheel problem apparently, but it is the cockpit indicator light at fault because the engineer climbs down underneath the flight deck, fiddles with something, and all is well.

Another smooth approach, full flap as we turn in over the fleets of ballasted tankers and the Russian fish factory vessels, a steep descent angle and we are down on the ground in a roar of reversed propeller blades.

A party led by the P&O agents greets us, and, while the others go to a hotel to relax, Bob Ward, Sammy Bradford and I are taken to Flag Officer Gibraltar for a gin and a quick briefing. I then pay my respects to the Medical Officer in Charge of the RN Hospital and we discuss likely routes of evacuation for casualities. The harbour below us is nearly empty in the evening sunlight, the storage depots in a similar state. The Gulf Task Force have just been through for replenishment before steaming south. Even for a Sunday, Gibraltar is strangely quiet.

Later on, under cover of darkness, the agent's cutter takes us out of the inner harbour and into a gentle swell. Suddenly she is there – a huge cathedral of lights that moves in close and then stops, waiting for us to come alongside. The rails crowded with passengers in evening dress, curious as the reason for this unscheduled diversion. They watch as seven young men with short haircuts and military bergans climb the rope-ladders lowered from a baggage port. Curiosity will later turn to anxiety when the rumour is leaked, deliberately,

24

that we are Customs Rummage Officers boarding early for the final part of the voyage.

In the Captain's beautifully appointed Day Cabin, Bob Ward breaks the news. There are sighs of relief that P&O will not have to fly all the passengers home there and then. In some of the officers I can detect excitement and anticipation; others, the ones with 1939-45 campaign medal ribbons, look more thoughtful and reflective. War, with its confusion, risk and danger, threatens their quiet and well-ordered lives once again.

April 5 – 6

A quick look around *Canberra's* public rooms, then a much slower and more careful inspection, confirms that there are only two possibilities for the medical areas. Our priorities must lie with wide open spaces and rapid access from a helicopter deck. Right aft lies the Peacock Room, with a swimming pool outside. The weight of steel girders and plates for a helo platform here will seriously affect the handling of the ship, so that idea has to be abandoned. The next choice involves a change in level, from the midships swimming pool or flight deck down into the starboard waist and along into the Stadium Theatre. That descent will pose problems for injured casualties, especially if they are on stretchers.

Canberra rolls and pitches in a choppy Bay of Biscay and the so-called sailor begins to feel sick. Dr Peter Mayner, the Ship's Surgeon, comes to my rescue with an intramuscular injection of Stemitil. He is a splendid character and, like the rest of the ship's officers and crew, cannot be more helpful and friendly as we try to imagine preparing their luxury liner for her troopship and floating hospital role. Our working relationship is so good in fact that we decide one lunch time to form the Canberra Medical Society! A social as well as scientific programme will hopefully ensure that all the medical, dental and nursing staff embarked are pointing their efforts in the same direction when war comes. I am to become a rather despotic chairman and Peter will organize the programme, while Susie West, Assistant Ship's Surgeon, 'volunteers' for the post of Treasurer. I also manage to book the massage parlour as the Medical Squadron office!

The final night at sea for the passengers who have circled the globe is a splendid affair. The dinner tables sag under multiple courses of tremendous standard and there is a lively cabaret to follow. Looking around the Stadium with its plush

26

fittings and thick carpet, it is very difficult to imagine bloodied operating tables and groaning wounded there. Are we really going to war? At the back of my mind I know the answer. All the rhetoric and diplomacy in the civilized world will not shift the Argentinian troops from the Falklands. We are going to have to push them off ourselves.

April 7 – 9

Southampton is a nightmare. *Canberra* is lying alongside a narrow wharf opened on to by a series of large baggage sheds. The drizzle falls from a leaden sky as the Vosper Thorneycroft men begin to cut metal and clear the upper deck fittings that will obstruct a helicopter's approach to the midships area. Tons of steel girders with mysterious chalk marks appear among the quayside jumble of freight and stores, are lifted carefully into the main swimming pool and bolted together. The weight of water in the pool has been calculated at 100 tons when full. The new steel forest will be about the same.

Ashore, Bob Ward and his men have worked out the loading plan and are now trying to convince the Army Port Liaison authorities to accept it. A senior Royal Marines captain has much the same background and experience as an Army major, but one chap doesn't quite understand this point. Bob asks for a half-hour break, makes a quick phone call to Plymouth and suddenly he's a major too, three months earlier than planned. Things proceed smoothly after that.

Along with the ammunition and other bits and pieces, boxes and boxes of medical stores are delivered and carefully netted and lifted up on to A Deck aft. The wharfies and crane drivers are tireless and cheerful but almost religious about tea breaks. Eventually, we realize they're right. Hot sweet tea at appropriate and regular intervals means more working hours in the end. A load of Argentinian corned beef is delivered, causing great hilarity among the working parties.

Piles of furnishings materialise from the bowels of the ship, all to be replaced later at the Ministry of Defence's expense. The Royal Marines of 40 and 42 Commando arrive, laden with kit, then 3 Para disembark from their buses, their camouflage smocks contrasting sharply with the blue dress uniforms of their Regimental band. On the medical side,

Surgeon Captain Roger Wilkes joins as Medical Officer in Charge. He is a general surgeon of wide experience, including action off Aden and Dar-es-Salaam during the Tanganyikan Rifles mutiny. We refer to him as FRW. John Williams is also on board as his deputy and we have a number of other surgeons, anaesthetists and general duties medical officers embarked specifically for *Canberra*.

To my surprise I discover that someone has ordered the Haslar SST to sail in HMS *Hermes*. It is a strange decision since they are supposedly dedicated to supporting the Royal Marines ashore, and have the appropriate equipment. 40 and 42 Commando's MOs are Surgeon Lieutenants Mike Hayward and Ross Adley. Mindful of our very recent chat in Norway I ask Ross where Crispin Swinhoe is. He says he cannot tell me. Then I realize that M Company are not on board either. Crispin has accompanied them, in a different ship, to retake South Georgia.

3 Para's MO is Captain John Burgess RAMC and he has, as reinforcement, a charming Ulsterman named John Graham, also a RAMC captain. There is a long-drawn-out saga as to whether or not RN nurses will join the ship. Eventually accommodation becomes so critical and space so tight that the problem boils down to 20 nurses or half a rifle company. All the girls are left behind, possibly to be flown out to us in Ascension, because the party of Vospers men still on board to finish the forward flight deck will have gone by then. In case that happens, Edith Meiklejohn, a Matron in the Queen Alexandra's Royal Navy Nursing Service and the deputy matron of Haslar, gets on board as advance guard.

Finally, unbelievably, everyone is over the brow, in a cabin and ready to go. As the sun dips below the horizon and light slowly fades, we cast off. The Para and Royal Marines bands strike up *Sailing* and *Land of Hope and Glory* as the liner edges out into Southampton Water. Cars honk horns and flash their headlights as *Canberra* gathers way, her decks lined with thoughtful men, some shedding silent tears as the town of Hamble slips slowly by down the port side. It is an emotional moment. How many of us will never see England again?

April 10 – 20

At sea, a routine begins to shape up. The men parade at 0830. We discuss the detail for the day then and try to integrate training requirements with the space available. The medical officers also meet, but separately under John Williams. Following this, John and I descend to C Deck for our morning brief with the Boss. FRW is a good host and has an amusing, original mind. In particular his memory for the detail of past events is incredible. When necessary we discuss signals that have come in and draft our replies. The 'crazy ideas' phase is obviously under way back in London. Some clever chap dusts off a pathology textbook and warns us about tick-and louse-borne diseases that are endemic to Argentina and therefore now liable to be encountered throughout the Falklands. John Williams, as a consultant physician, gently enquires how substantial this conclusion can be in view of the cold and wet conditions prevailing there, compared with the hot dry pampas. *I* think that lead poisoning will be a greater hazard! Other signals fly around in response, demanding gallons of disinfectant and delousing powder by the first available air drop.

John Williams also gets going on working up *Canberra's* action medical organization. He beavers away, filling a large bound book with clinical policy notes and sudden ideas which eventually distil into two concise typewritten pages. Drama ensues one day when the book is 'lost', to be returned by a sticky-fingered culprit soon after John makes a broadcast to the ship emphasizing the nature of its contents.

There are arguments over priorities for training areas, fuelled by ignorance among some of the embarked military about our role. We are aware that we are travelling southwards with our potential customers and anxious not to point that out too bluntly, but a few of the Para and Royal Marine officers refuse to see beyond the end of their own training programmes. I settle one bootneck captain's hash by suggesting that if he protests further about 'bloody medics' I'll arrange for him to be admitted to Minor Treatments when we go to war, however serious his injuries. All of a sudden, he sees my point.

Alongside us, the men of the Commando Forces Band train as hard as anyone. Gradually they absorb all the minor military jobs on board until finally they have a range of 28 different skills on offer, in addition to the playing of their music which they do so well. They are a tremendous asset with their willingness and good humour as well as going right in there when it comes to the practical side of stretcher bearing and first aid training.

Alternate evenings see the Canberra Medical Society under way, launched with great success by the annual cocktail party in Peter Mayner's cabin. It is an excellent evening with barriers broken down on all sides between hospital types and the general duties boys. FRW is in particularly good form and manages to silence Ross Adley completely for a few minutes, an incredible feat, with this exchange:

Adley: 'With all due respect, sir . . .'

FRW: 'Listen lad, don't *ever* use that phrase with me. I've been on enough Sick Bay runs ashore in my time to know it *always* precedes an insult.'

We invite Lieutenant Colonel Hew Pike to speak about Airborne Forces, then wine and dine with him and his centurions – the company commanders of 3 Para as our guests. There is similar treatment for the officers of 40 and 42 Commandos, in return for talks about the Corps and Arctic operations respectively by their COs, Malcolm Hunt and Nick Vaux. Gradually their collective reservations disappear, along with our difficulties about training areas. About this time we also make the first emergency pipe: 'For exercise, for exercise. Casualities inbound within the hour. Rig emergency medical facilities.'

The boys turn to with a will, operating tables and anaesthetic trolleys appearing from storage places all around the Stadium. Arctic camouflage netting gets strung from the deckhead to divide off the various areas, stores and stretchers are laid out, and the Bonito Night Club actually begins to look like a ward. Soon the timings are down to Field Gun levels as the participants become more practised.

Overnight on April 17 we are lying alongside the refuelling jetty at Freetown, a rather scruffy-looking port in Sierra Leone. There is some suspicion that the Government has only allowed *Canberra* to refuel there because she is basically a hospital ship. If the local British Consul is, therefore, a little surprised to see several thousand 'male nurses' on board, he says nothing, and merely contents himself with a tour of the emergency medical areas. Luckily, we have left everything rigged for a night practice, to test the lighting systems. Long before dawn we are at sea again, heading for the Equator.

Ascension Island. Huge piles of brown and blue-grey volcanic dust rise steeply in the centre of the island to a cooler, vegetation-covered feature aptly named Green Mountain. Rear Admiral Woodward's main battle fleet has sailed, but around us on the bright blue sea lie the anchored ships of the landing force, including a large American oiler. The water teems with unattractive little black fish that apparently possess piranha-like qualities. The stories about the size of these predators grow in the telling and I am seriously questioned by one of the journalists on board as to the identity of some unlucky Task Force bather who has actually been torn to pieces by them! An occasional hammerhead shark lazily flaps by, the sunlight dappling on the grey back as its dorsal fin creases the surface swell. Helicopters, landing craft and Mexeflotes busy themselves with tactical restowage. Most of the stores had been loaded higgledy-piggledy into ships to meet the sailing deadline from Plymouth, and much effort is expanded now in getting the right mix of combat supplies into the correct ships for the landing. The LSL *Sir Lancelot* is hot and stuffy but the boys of 1 Medical Troop are cheerful. Their boss, Malcolm Hazell, has displayed his lunatic enthusiasm for road running by actually completing a *marathon* distance on a small 60-yard circuit of her cramped deck. It is a tremendous effort of stamina, especially as the LSLs possess the stable qualities of a drunken corkscrew in anything other than dry dock.

Training continues. From dawn to dusk the Marines and Paras grind round and round *Canberra*'s quarter mile of Promenade Deck in heavy-booted, muscular and sweating squads. Some of them are now carrying loaded bergans, or machine guns and anti-tank weapons to increase the punishment. The company commanders, worried about the repetitive nature of some of the classroom work, press anxiously for a chance to get ashore, march in a straight line for once and also zero their infantry and support wagons. Over the two-week period we are there everyone gets that chance and it is gratefully taken. One remarkable day 3 Para's anti-tank platoon fire 37½ training years' worth of Wombat ammunition. Even the medics manage a march across the Island, from English Bay to Wideawake Airfield. The hot tarmac means blisters for me after five miles, but the pain is well worth it. Peter Mayner comes with us, as do some of the Naval Medical Assistants who are not Commando-trained, but cope surprisingly well in spite of this.

On the range I watch the Brigade Staff fire their pistols in practice, then see their renewed efforts after an ex-SAS officer attached to Julian Thompson's staff gives them a short demonstration. It is the most effective piece of military tuition I've ever seen, but surely something will be badly wrong if the Brigade Commander ever has to fire his 9mm Browning in self-defence! Overhead, Hercules transports, Victor tankers and Sea Harrier fighters keep the normally sleepy airfield circuit busy.

On several occasions I also take advantage of the empty co-pilot's seat in *Canberra*'s resident Sea King Commando helicopter. Ron Crawford or Martin Eales are happy to have someone to talk to, and let me fly many of the sectors as we practise airborne assaults from *Canberra* to Wideawake's main dispersal. Some of the boys in the back are not so happy when they recognize me, and see just whose hands are on the cyclic and collective.

The weather is glorious and flying exhilarating. The Vulcan which has put Port Stanley's airfield out of action* is parked near the main traffic building, an armed sentry guarding it. On one circuit back to the anchored fleet we hear 'Mayday Mayday . . . engine failure' and there below me, a Gazelle suddenly arrives on the beach in a flurry of sand and slowing rotor blades. Martin takes control and executes a quick spiralling descent down to it. We confirm that all is well with the pilot and observer, and although the skids are deeply buried the aircraft itself appears undamaged.

* This is what we believed at the time.

Another afternoon is exciting for a different reason. On *Elk*, a crewman develops sudden and severe abdominal pain. The Duty Medical Officer from *Canberra* goes to the aft pontoon and gets into a landing craft. Unfortunately he also forgets which ship called for help, and spends the afternoon touring the fleet. Peter Mayner hears on the P&O grapevine that one of 'his' crewmen is ill, so he commandeers a rigid raider. Finally a Wessex helicopter arrives on deck, with some stores and offers to help. Without knowing what is happening elsewhere, I board the aircraft and descend to *Elk*'s main deck and find that Peter has already arrived, soaking wet after his high-speed ride, and that the crewman is obviously very unwell. He's probably perforated a duodenal ulcer and a boat journey back to *Canberra* would be cruel, and probably lethal. We carefully winch him up into the Wessex cabin, transfer him as smoothly as possible and an hour later Phil Shouler is working inside his belly. The diagnosis is confirmed and the hole neatly oversewn – some real surgery at last.

May 7

We have sailed. Hooray. From my frequent visits to *Fearless*, I hear on the grapevine that the number of landing options has dropped from eight to three and a final selection is imminent. My friendly Staff Officer in charge of medical matters in Brigade is a genial Royal Marines major named Gerry Wells-Cole, a man who would normally be oiling his cricket bat at this time of the year, ready for the start of the season. Already annoyed by the unauthorised removal of the Portsmouth SST from his Order of Battle, he now finds himself the subject of conflicting advice from another source, someone who has no experience with the Corps or its medical support. Our normal system of command and control is in danger of being interfered with, so we try to carry on in pursuit of common sense and maximum effectiveness.

Medically, the plot is clearing. The word is still that *Canberra* will be close in to any Force landing area, and with Roger Wilkes' excellent organization now at a high pitch of efficiency, the Royal Marines' element of medical support will remain both integrated and embarked. We will, however, retain our capability of going ashore when and if the battle dictates. My private worries about the air threat seem to be shared by all the Brigade Staff, but apparently the Naval Task Force will have air superiority established by the time we get down to the Total Exclusion Zone.

Uganda has joined us but is causing problems. The ship's sophisticated communications kit has been stripped out to meet the terms of the Geneva Convention and, apart from satellite communications, there are very few ways in which we can talk to her. Indeed, a policy of severe restriction in electronic transmissions has now been imposed. The Argentinians will undoubtedly be listening and trying to fix our position. What a juicy target *Canberra* would be for one of their three remaining submarines on a long-range mission!

Poor *Uganda* seems rather out of it and no one seems sure of her role. Will she float 600 miles out, using the converted survey ships, *Hydra*, *Hecla* and *Herald* as hospital carriers to bring patients out to her? Edith Meiklejohn leaves us to become Matron of *Uganda*, and FRW escorts her across and looks around the big white hospital ship.

On *Canberra*, harmony is the name of the game. The specialist training for the embarked surgeons, in particular, is of a very high order. As well as receiving tutorials from the Boss, they repeatedly watch and discuss excerpts from a consignment of Vietnam and Korean medical training films that arrived on board in Ascension. It is a nice mixture of practical and realistic advice, combined with Technicolour fantasy. The boys are raring to go, well prepared and pretty confident.

May 11

This morning I fly over to *Norland*, the P&O North Sea ferry that also joined us in Ascension. She carries the 2nd Battalion of the Parachute Regiment, as well as the medical men of the Parachute Clearing Troop. Phil Shouler and John Williams fly to HMS *Intrepid* which has also rejoined the Fleet after an incredibly rapid mini-refit in Portsmouth. Somebody has suggested the conversion of her wardroom and gunroom into a surgical operating theatre. Indeed, work has actually begun on cutting away bulkheads before Phil and John can stop them. To reach the wardroom by stretcher from the flight deck requires the negotiation of two sharp corners and a vertical companionway, or ladder. It is palpable nonsense.

Norland tells a different story. Space is cramped, but the new flight deck aft opens into a large public room that is close to the existing operating theatre. The PCT personnel are all parachute-trained, and practise their role regularly. The Medical Officers, even the surgeons and anaesthetists, have all been Battalion MOs at some time and therefore have a close affinity with and affection for the 'Toms', as they call the private soldiers.

Steve Hughes, the young RAMC Captain who is 2 Para's Regimental MO, has been very, very busy. He is a real enthusiast, receptive to other people's ideas and determined that *his* first aid training and preparation will be the best. Having read about soldiers in the Israeli Army each carrying a bag of intravenous fluid, he realizes that this is the way to solve his stores problem in the field. Each paratrooper will carry his own bag of fluid and some of the patrol medics are trained to insert intravenous needles. For the others, in case they are cut off from medical help, he demonstrates the principle of rectal infusion. The Toms laugh, and volunteer each other for this procedure. None of them have yet heard of a place called Goose Green.

Thursday, May 13

The pace is quickening. A decision has been made and in the afternoon key officers are called to *Fearless* for Brigadier Thompson's landing 'O' Group. As his medical adviser I go along too, and as we take our seats in the LPD's crowded Wardroom we are all conscious that this is an historic event. The briefing for Suez, 25 years ago, must have been something like this.

There is a lot of preliminary information to get through. The weather and terrain are covered once again by Major Ewen Southby-Tailyour with his excellent portfolio of slides and cruising notes. He looks thinner and more tired than his usual extrovert self. The strain of being responsible for finding a Force Landing Site has obviously been telling.

An immaculately delivered Intelligence Brief follows from Captain Viv Rowe, a tall, fair-haired and strongly built veteran of operations in Muscat and Oman. There are gaps, however, particularly as to the capability of the Fuerza Aerea Argentina.

The Brigadier stands up, looks for a moment at the Commanding Officers sitting in the chintz-covered front-row chairs, dons his spectacles and in a quiet but clear voice gives his orders: 'Mission, gentlemen. To land in Port San Carlos, San Carlos Settlement and Ajax Bay, and establish a beachhead for mounting offensive operations leading to the recapture of the Falkland Islands.'

There is absolute silence. He repeats the sentence, then carries on: 'Design for battle. A *silent*, night attack by landing craft, with the object of securing all high ground by first light –'

The crisp instructions follow, one by one, until every angle and problem is covered. Many of the details are classified Secret and still remain so, but eventually all the questions are answered, either by the Brigadier himself, or by the Brigade

Major, John Chester. There is a rustle of papers as people make preparations to leave, anxious to write their own orders as soon as possible

'*Gentlemen!*', Julian Thompson's voice has a whiplash edge as his narrowed eyes scan the audience: 'May I remind you again – this will be no picnic.'

Saturday, May 15

A rough day. We now have a little more information about the San Carlos area, including the location of any large buildings suitable for setting up our expanded dressing stations. On the western edge of San Carlos Water lies a shallow indentation called Ajax Bay, now codenamed Red Beach. Just up from the beach is a large mutton refrigeration and packing plant. Built as a joint venture between the Falkland Islands Company and the British Government, it seems to have foundered because of a lack of local labour, and has lain abandoned since the late 1950s. Ajax Bay looks like becoming the main logistic support area so part of the mutton plant is pencilled in on the Brigade chart as a potential site for Medical Squadron when they disembark from *Canberra* and *Sir Lancelot*.

Anxiety persists about *Canberra* as the only reasonable surgical facility, so Phil Shouler continues his wanderings around the fleet, this time travelling to the Fleet Stores Ship, RFA *Stromness*. Erich Bootland, the new OC of 3 Troop, keeps him company and they quickly assess *Stromness*'s total unsuitability for handling emergency cases in any volume. The deck waist areas are certainly wide enough for patients, but they are also piled high with stores, and the fork-lift trucks need space to get around the crates and boxes. Phil and Erich have to spend the night on board, doubling up with some of the officers of 45 Commando. It is an uncomfortable experience after *Canberra*. Her propeller shafts vibrate badly each time the stern rises out of the water, before slamming back down into the next wave with a crash that shakes the whole ship. For the medical support to 3rd Commando Brigade, *Canberra* is still number one, with *Norland* as the only practical alternative.

Feeling queasy myself, despite *Canberra*'s stabilizers, I manage to keep down enough Stugeron to give the operatio-

41

nal and landing brief to the senior medical men. For security reasons we are in FRW's cabin which is below the Promenade Deck. The horizon keeps vanishing from the large panoramic windows so the Boss kindly draws the curtains, seeing that otherwise the audience will probably get more than just information on their notebooks.

Sunday, May 16

A quieter day, thank goodness, and a calmer sea. Terry Knott, the Second in Command of the Logistics Regiment, comes on board for a look around. He is a tall, slim Royal Marines major who won the Military Cross in Aden as a young and lethal subaltern. Unlucky enough to be in Denmark on a recce when Galtieri invaded the Falklands, he was recalled rapidly but then left behind to look after the rear party. Repeated letters and daily threatening phone calls around the Corps bazaars resulted in a late regain, and now he is in charge of a composite rifle company on board *Intrepid*. I'm glad to see him, and as a result of a long chat am able to write an accurate medical operation order.

The blood-taking sessions are now complete. Trying to estimate casualty numbers and their likely degrees of seriousness is a very difficult business when there are so many unknown variables in the equation. The pathologists also reckon that we'll be able to store fresh blood in the special Fenwal plastic transfusion bags for about five weeks, providing the low temperature in the special chilling boxes is carefully maintained.

Each of the three embarked Units is invited to participate as donors. There must be some sort of inter-unit rivalry going, because eventually the doctors are turning away potential donors. We have over 1,000 half-litre bags of high-quality red stuff on tap. Although the men only get warm lemonade as a rehydrating reward for their contribution to the mutual life insurance policy, they'll make up the lost red cells before we land. The timing of these sessions has been a tricky piece of judgement for FRW.

Monday, May 17

Clearance is signalled from *Fearless* to begin briefing audiences about the landing plan, down to junior NCO level. The Boss suggests, correctly, that we start with our medical, dental and para-medical officers as well as the command structure of the Band. Fleet Chief Dobbs, my Medical Administration Officer, and a Naval medical branch rating of over 17 years service with the Corps, describes the Naval part of the landing plan to an attentive audience. He is a tremendous character and has a wicked sense of humour too:

'I spy, with my little eye, something beginning with E . . . and you've got six seconds to answer.'*

* Exocet.

Tuesday, May 18

Today it's the turn of Medical Squadron, the Surgical Support Teams and the Band to get the facts. The Bonito Room is full as once more we run through the brief, which is now fairly polished. *Canberra* is still 80 miles outside the TEZ so D-Day has not yet been finalized. *I* know when we are due to land but am not allowed to divulge the date. Most of the boys work it out for themselves anyway.

The first 'war' casualty is also received on board. An idle idiot of a fire sentry in *Europic Ferry* plays with a grenade detonator. Out of boredom he removes the pin, then tries to replace it. The explosion blows several fingers off and drives metal fragments into face and chest. Phil Jones and Nick Morgan do a beautiful tidying-up job.

In the evening, frantic pipes on the tannoy indicate that something is up. It turns out that Brigade are very worried about the submarine and air threat to our ship. With two Commando units and one Para battalion on board *Canberra*, they definitely have the majority of their assault troop eggs in one large white basket. Plans are made to cross deck 40 Commando and 3 Para into other ships tomorrow.

Wednesday, May 19

A beautiful morning, with clear skies and only a light swell to interfere with the difficult business of transferring 40 Commando to *Fearless*, and, later, 3 Para to *Intrepid*. The marines and soldiers wear their full assault gear for the operation, leaving their suitcases and other personal kit in the baggage store rooms. Some of the smaller individuals are dwarfed by their loaded bergans. The medics are rather more heavily laden than most since they have to tote ammunition *and* medical stores. Top weight is carried by the mortar and anti-tank sections. A 81mm mortar barrel, plus personal equipment, weighs 60 kg. Bergan, fighting order, weapon, ammunition and a Milan firing post clock in at an amazing, and back-breaking, 64 kg!

I spend a busy day packing morphine syrettes for the various sub-units on a scale of one per man. The estimates are difficult because some units, like the gunners of 29 Commando Regiment Royal Artillery, are scattered between four or five ships. I get most of the stuff delivered before nightfall and ask for a Gazelle helicopter next day to complete the issues.

Tragedy strikes after dark as a Sea King helicopter crashes, killing most of the passengers as it hits the sea. There are rumours of impact with a large bird, causing the anti-icing shield to break up into both engines. The buzz also is that the passengers were all SAS men – later confirmed. It is a bitter blow since among them are the battle-tested hard men of South Georgia and Pebble Island. May they rest in peace.

Thursday, May 20

The 18-ship Landing Force forms up and penetrates the TEZ at dawn. We are 200 miles east of Port Stanley and the gods are kind to us. A Force Six wind and sea state are combined with thick mist that hides us from the prying eyes of Argentinian aircraft. Long-range radar indicates that the enemy are certainly out looking for us, but the Sea Harriers sitting at Alert on *Hermes*' long flight deck have no close customers to intercept. The Seawolf-equipped frigates, HMS *Broadsword* and *Brilliant*, fuss around on the flanks of the convoy as it ploughs steadily westwards. The LSLs are rolling and pitching badly, their wide bows often obliterated in a foaming mass of freezing South Atlantic. Helicoper flying is also very difficult, so my morphine issue by Gazelle is cancelled. Problems for me, as a result, but I will have to try a final distribution run on D-Day. We have agreed that there will be no casualty evacuation (casevac) facilities after the H-Hour landings, at least until first light, when I will have a Wessex helicopter dedicated to the Brigade for casevac purposes.

The 'longest day' drags on and on, until night falls at last. Precisely on time, the Landing Force convoy turns north and begins the long right hook up to the top of Falkland Sound. One of the escorts carries straight on and helps to distract Argentinian curiosity by bombarding Port Stanley together with HMS *Glamorgan*. We also know that tonight another group of SAS men will be making a lot of explosive and diversionary noises near Goose Green, further confusing the defending forces.

Most of us turn in early as D-Day will be a long one. As I dress for bed in survival clothing the BBC World Service describes how an amphibious landing in the Falklands is now imminent. They even have a tame expert to describe what will happen. The 'former Director of Naval Intelligence' is hopelessly wrong when he describes landing craft as out-dated, and that the assault helicopters will either land in Port Stanley or on the plains of Lafonia. He also states that in his opinion the assault will not be a bloody affair. With the poor casevac facilities at our disposal during the hours of darkness, I sincerely hope that at least he's got *something* right.

Friday, May 21

Loud bangs, in pairs, wake me up. The noises have a brassy, metallic sound and seem very close. Pulling down the black-out curtain on the cabin scuttle reveals a bright flash occurring before each sound. Then I remember. HMS *Antrim* is providing naval gunfire support for the attack on Fanning Head. An Argentine OP has been spotted in the area and the SBS are due in there as soon as a dose of 4.5 inch warheads have been dispensed.

Putting on more warm clothing, I walk up to the midships flight deck and step out of the red-lit corridor into the chilly darkness. It takes a few minutes to gain night vision. The stars of the southern night sky are brilliant and unfamiliar but all around is complete blackness. I have brought my binoculars and am feeling my way up to the Officer's sun deck on the port side when *Antrim* opens up again. From my vantage point the noise is almost painful. The thunderclap of each firing rolls unchecked over the flat calm of Falkland Sound, and each one follows a long yellow tongue of flame that briefly stabs out into the darkness. Two, maybe three, seconds later there is a distant 'Kerr-ump' as the shells impact *terra firma* on Fanning Head. We are at anchor while the initial assault goes in from *Norland*, *Fearless* and *Intrepid*, but the plan is to move *Canberra* into San Carlos Water around first light.

Breakfast tastes good, anxiety about today's programme of events fuelling my appetite. The stewards are subdued, although *Antrim*'s percussion section is inaudible down here in the Pacific Restaurant.

The first fingers of light appear in the east as we move silently under Fanning Head to our anchor position. The two picks go down with a tumble of chain from the bows and I find myself standing next to Nick Vaux who is obviously fretful at being held in reserve for the initial assault. From the bridge, in the lightening gloom, we can make out the shapes of the two LSLs gliding past, then the familiar outline of *Stromness*. Over on Fanning Head a machine gun opens up silently, the red tracer blips streaking in a long curving arc before bouncing and ricocheting at the base of the hill. The SBS are in a fire fight, but it all seems a bit one-sided.

Dawn breaks imperceptibly, the violet layers next to the skyline gradually brightening through deep indigo and blue, then orange as the sun's disc rises. It is going to be a clear blue sky. Good for our helicopters certainly, but also wonderful flying weather for any Argentinian Air Force planes hunting us. They *must* have spotted the landing force fleet by now.

On cue, and on time, The Sea Kings begin to line up in the hover out to *Canberra*'s port. Their Rolls-Royce Gnome engines have a characteristic whistling roar which is blended to the nasal whine of the six-bladed tail rotor. You can shut your eyes but still be sure of correct identification by listening. The netted loads of first- and second-line ammunition are lifted ashore beneath their boat-shaped fuselages. In the clearer light we can now see little groups of landing craft streaming past, taking 3 Para into Port San Carlos. They are about an hour late but this seems to be the only hitch in an amphibious assault which has otherwise gone like clockwork.

The Ops Room is busy but the airwaves are silent. No one can tell me if the landings were opposed or not. If there are casaulties then Steven Hughes, John Burgess, David Griffiths and Mike Hayward will simply have to do their best until I can arrive after dawn with the means to get them out.

An hour after sun-up there is still no sign of the Wessex, but then suddenly Mike Crabtree and his crew are there. They are marshalled on to the forward deck and then shut down. They have already been flying for more than three hours after inserting the SBS and their kit into Fanning Head, so a quick cup of coffee is in order before we depart.

The run down to San Carlos Settlement is uneventful as Mike checks the map and Hector, the co-pilot, flies the aircraft. Turning into wind, we land on Falklands soil for the first time and I run over to the nearest men who are digging slit trenches. Some of the blackened faces are recognizable as

Marines of 40 Commando who reassure me that the landing on Blue Beach has been uneventful. Two children run out to look at the Wessex, this new phenomenon in their lives, so I go over to say hello. They are chubby-cheeked and pink-faced, and one shyly gives me a sweet. I grin and jerk my thumb at the helicopter. The elder smiles, reaches into her anorak and gives me another Murraymint – this one for the pilot.

Next we fly to Red Beach, the Brigade codename for Ajax Bay, and land on a convenient piece of concrete hardstanding. Our reception here is much less friendly One of 45's Corporals invites us to investigate sex and travel as he thinks that they are being mortared. No casualties here either apparently, but we need no second bidding. The Wessex rises swiftly and turns over the deserted refrigeration plant. Jock Inglis, one of my Marines, has told me that the abandoned freezing rooms are big enough to play football in. Interesting, but it will probably take some time to get read as a field medical facility or dressing station, and hopefully the highly capable action medical organization in *Canberra* will be all that we need.

As we climb away I have time to notice a few details. Along the front of the main building, which is shaped like a 'T', there is a narrow concrete track. This road leads down to a broken pier, past a huge stack of red and rusting oil drums. The ground looks horrible – wet, muddy and very stony.

After refuelling on *Fearless* we distribute the last of the morphine to the various ships. Minutes after returning to *Canberra*, the first casevac request comes in. The grid reference makes little sense until we ask for it to be repeated, and then find that the figures are in a form of code that we don't possess! Some rummaging in the adjoining Ops Room provides the correct answer, and away we go. Right at the head of San Carlos Water we see a discharging red smoke grenade land on the shore nearby, and it's a chap from 2 Para who has badly twisted his back falling down into a ditch.

Corporal Gleeson, the aircrewman, rips out the cabin seats to make a crude stretcher on to which we gently lift the injured man. It seems a crazy thing to do, but in the morning sunlight I step back to take a picture of this historic event.

There is another task waiting when we return to *Canberra* but this turns into a wild goose chase. The saga ends when we query the grid reference, only to find that it is the first set of numbers once more but wrongly de-coded. While refuelling on *Fearless* again, I race up to the Brigade Ops Room to protest. I ask the Duty Officer responsible for us to give casevac positions in 'clear' from now on and the anti-flash hooded figure agrees.

My remonstrations attract the attention of the Officer Commanding Special Boat Squadron. He is desperate to visit his men up on Fanning Head but cannot find a helicopter. Apparently there are some casualties there too, so I offer him the ride, which is gratefully accepted. He grabs his Armalite rifle and, after strapping in, we lift again. Seconds later we have a new task.

There has been an incident involving helicopters up near Port San Carlos Settlement. We race up to the scene but apparently get too close to the forward edge of the battle area. Mike suddenly notices paratroopers, in attacking formation, advancing beneath him. He pulls the Wessex around again in a diving turn that brings us very close to the sea. Having beaten a hasty retreat, we collect our senses once more. A closer look at the map, a slower approach, and we are suddenly on top of the reported incident. Mike lands into wind but says nothing. OC SBS and I get out to see what is going on, and are greeted by an horrendous sight. Its back broken and its cockpit contents strewn over the grass, a Gazelle of the Brigade Air Squadron lies on the ground. The two paratroopers who stayed behind have done all they can, but to no avail. The pilot and air gunner are dead, their flying suits stained with blood.

We pick up the bodies and carry them back to the Wessex, removing the machine gun and the pilot's camera from the wreckage. I'd met Ken Francis several times back in Coypool and flown with him as well. Our hearts are heavy as we fly our two dead colleagues back to *Canberra* and I hand down the camera to Fleet Chief Dobbs.

Next, we fly up to Fanning Head. There are three Argentine wounded to evacuate after Mike has done a little stores shifting job for the SBS Troop. The conscript prisoners look terrified, apparently believing the stories that the British will eat them if they are captured. I decide to take the injured amongst them to *Canberra* because, although there are orders saying prisoners should not be flown in helicopters, there is nowhere else for them to go. Perhaps, also, if Buenos Aires is told that Argentinian wounded are being treated in *Canberra* they will leave the liner alone.

I take some more photos and we fly back to *Canberra* in two trips, because cabin floor space for stretchers is very limited. The Argentinian lads have all got high-velocity gunshot wounds of the legs so they will definitely need surgery.

Somewhere around midday the casevac tasks are temporarily complete so Mike Crabtree elects to refuel once more and return to *Canberra*'s forward deck. With its nylon lashings now secured, the big Wessex helicopter's four blades slow to a halt and the engines are shut down at last.

Deep in the bowels of the ship, life goes on normally. The Pacific Restaurant is being cleared after lunch but the staff arrange a quick resupply of rolls and ham for me and the crew. Up in the Stadium, things have been more hectic as resuscitation and assessment of numerous casualties continue against a background of repeated air raids and tannoy warnings to take cover.

As I walk from the Stadium through to the Bonito, the metallic voices booms out: 'This is the bridge. Attack developing from the north . . . Two aircraft . . . TAKE COVER . . . TAKE COVER!' All around me people drop, poleaxed, to the shiny corridor floors. Pressing ourselves into an unyielding surface, arms clutched tightly in protection over our heads, we can hear the reverberating echo of the machine guns on the bridge superstructure as they engage the attackers. The noise is like a road mender's drill and seems amplified as it carries through the ship's aluminium superstructure. There is a sudden 'Whoosh' – the Argentinian jet going past? 'Blowpipe,' mutters someone in the dim passageway.

Shortly afterwards the 'all clear' is given and I am munching my ham roll when the next tannoy order is given. 'Launch the casevac helicopter . . . I say again, Launch the casevac helicopter . . .' Captain Chris Burne, *Canberra*'s Senior Naval Officer, gives a brief situation report, much appreciated by his 2,000-strong and entirely captive audience. HMS *Argonaut* has been damaged in an air attack and is asking for help with her injured.

On the forward flight deck the lashings are off the Wessex by the time I arrive up there, and Mike Crabtree has already started one engine. Moments later we are 'burning and turning', then we ease into the air and away again. The helicopter takes a direct line to the damaged Leander Class frigate, easily visible as she curves around Fanning Head towards the north end of Falkland Sound, her funnel smoking more heavily than usual.

Mike positions the Wessex over her boiling wake with the starboard door looking down to an empty flight deck. Donning the winch strop and sitting on the cabin doorstep, all seems clear for my transfer, but the Flight Deck Officer stubbornly refuses us. His arms remain crossed instead of beckoning in the Wessex with his bats. The stand-off continues for ages – probably a minute or more, then the aircrewman taps me on the shoulder, unplugs my helmet electrical lead and swings me up and out of the aircraft to begin the short descent to the flight deck, fifteen feet below. The Wessex moves sideways and over the deck, then suddenly dips its bulbous nose towards the sea and begins to accelerate away.

I curse Mike Crabtree's lack of concern for my welfare and struggle to regain the cabin. By now we are pulling round to the left in a tight turn at low level, really moving fast over the waves. Plugging in again, I have no time to complain. The crewman sees and hears me join the intercom circuit and says briefly, 'Air Raid Red, sir, enemy aircraft coming in.'

Kneeling by the doorway again, my pulse racing, I notice that we are crossing a small beach under Fanning Head and, as the nose rears up now to slow the aircraft, I look out. Two menacing shapes flash overhead, the stubby delta wings easily recognizable as A4 Skyhawks. As we settle in a small gully to take stock the air seems full of snow. It is 'chaff', metallized nylon fibres thrown up by *Argonaut* in a last-ditch attempt to deflect the oncoming attackers. A little later Mike Crabtree lifts the Wessex and moves off along the hillside, following the line of a stream down a small re-entrant. At one point the gully widens out about 600 feet above sea level and with some careful precision hovering he is able to position the starboard main wheel on the raised bank of the stream. The cabin machinegun can now be swung in a wide defensive arc of fire which will not intersect with the spinning rotor blades. More attacks are developing on the Naval picket line in Falkland Sound, so we settle down to watch, as well as wait for the chance to get airborne again.

The tactical net is busy as various ships call the developing air strikes. Every now and then our faces split in wide grins as the net controller in HMS *Brilliant* announces another downed Argentinian aircraft. The Sea Harriers, on Combat Air Patrol, are proving lethal to the Mirages and Skyhawks on their way back to the mainland. Their successes come as a laconic 'CAP – Splash one A-4' but to the picket line and the Landing Force ships in San Carlos the words mean tremendous encouragement.

In the distance we can see another attack begin on the ships at the southern end of the Sound. A black dot appears above the horizon, then dips, swooping in low and fast and leaving two towering plumes of water where its bombs have straddled one of the frigates. The dot is now recognisable as a jet fighter which climbs up and away, twisting and weaving to make good its escape. Too late. A thin white line joins HMS *Broadsword*'s foredeck to the fleeing aircraft, and it silently explodes, disolving into metal confetti. Corporal Kevin Gleeson and I clap each other on the back with excitement and laughter. Our headphones crackle again: 'Four hostiles . . . 070 twenty miles and closing fast.' Kneeling on the cabin floor I hang out of the doorway for a better look but to the north east there is nothing but blue sky and puffy white clouds.

As I swing back in to check the bearing, Corporal Gleeson points upwards past my shoulder. From the north, accelerating as they dive, four Mirages begin an attack on HMS *Antrim*. Like a mother tiger prowling restlessly in the neck of San Carlos Water as she protects her cubs behind, the big guided missile destroyer spits back her defiance. The line of splashes caused by Mirage cannon shells now meets her tall grey flanks and for several seconds she absorbs hundreds of direct hits.

The fourth Mirage has other ideas. Disturbed by the rising

cloud of red tracer, he breaks off left and straightens up, heading directly for us. Corporal Gleeson cocks the GPMG and begins to fire upwards at the lethal outline that we now see expanding rapidly. Are the leading edges of the Mirage twinkling with cannon fire? My decision is reflex. Jumping down, I dive straight into the ditch. Better a clean death here from a 30mm shell through the head than incineration and fragmentation in a whirling maelstrom of ruptured fuel tanks and broken rotor blades . . .

But the end does not come in the blinding flash of agony that I am half ready for. Instead, the Wessex is still sitting noisily behind me, and there is no sign of the Mirage. Once again the skies are clear and *Antrim* begins another turn in her endless race track pattern.

Picking myself out of the ditch I notice that one trouser leg is wet and muddy and my helmet visor has jammed down after its violent contact with the ground. Climbing back up into the cabin, I am ignored by Kevin Gleeson as he makes the machine gun safe. Mike Crabtree's first words to me as I plug back in have a faintly sarcastic ring: 'Oh, you back with us, Doc?' He and his crew have had to remain strapped in throughout the incident. I feel very ashamed and humbled at my terror in the face of the enemy.

Down on the beach, there is movement near the water's edge as two heads suddenly pop up above the surface. Frogmen? No, just two seals that play among the kelp beds for a few moments, then dive again to escape the crazy antics of man.

In Falkland Sound, the Royal Navy's picket line of frigates continues its tremendous and courageous fight against the Argentinian Air Force. More dots above the horizon, a distant flash and smoke, and we cheer again, thinking that Seawolf has gobbled up another victim. But then the tactical net spits out the four-letter call sign of the ship that has been hit. It is HMS *Ardent* that we can see at the base of that column of smoke.

Mike and I feel that we must go to her assistance, but are unsure whether or not it is safe to get into the air again. The answer comes immediately as a Naval Wasp helicopter rushes past us, nose down for maximum speed, as it transits to *Canberra* with a casualty from *Argonaut*. The Fleet Air Arm pilot has obviously decided that the requirement for his services exceeds the risk of providing them. His unsung but inspired bravery is just what we need at that critical moment. Mike lifts the collective lever, swings out over the beach and soon we are filling our near-empty fuel tanks on *Fearless*.

I run to the main ramp area leading down to the Tank Deck and grab two new-looking, winchable stretchers. The Chief Petty Officer of the Flight Deck comes over to query my actions but waves me on my way as soon as he hears that *Ardent* has been hit. A true sailor will give everything he has for a brother seafarer in distress. We take the direct route around to the scene of *Ardent*'s bombing, climbing to cross the Sussex Mountains south of Ajax Bay. It is ground still held by the enemy as far as we know, so Mike, a Commando helicopter instructor, hugs the contours of the ground as we speed along.

Over the hump and descending, we in the back are denied the sight at which they fall silent up in the cockpit. Downwind of the burning ship the acrid smell pervades the cabin as we fly through a thick pall of black smoke. The Wessex comes to a hover again, 30 feet above the swell and just off *Ardent*'s port quarter. Now silenced ourselves, the crewman and I stare out.

What a sight! The Type 21 frigate lies still in the water, listing and drifting. Her lovely, classic lines have been obscenely defaced by some demented giant who has smashed her helicopter hangar and opened up the flight deck edge with a huge tin opener. Deep inside the enormous blackened hole with its ragged edges, the fires of Hell are burning. The flames have a bright orange intensity that is painful to look at directly. Reaching for my camera once again, to photograph the blazing wound, I find to my disgust that there are no exposures left. While I am looking for another film, Mike Crabtree and his crew notice that *Ardent*'s survivors are now grouped on the upper works, forward of the bridge. Some are already in their Day-Glo emergency survival suits, but almost all of them are pointing at the sea off the port bow.

Mike spots two survivors in the water and moves the

Wessex across. As a passenger, I have no part to play in their retrieval, so continue searching for a fresh roll of film in my various pockets and watch the seamanship of HMS *Yarmouth*'s captain as he puts her bows next to *Ardent*'s so that survivors can simply step across. But then Corporal Gleeson seems to be having trouble with the first survivor. I crawl over to the cabin door, look down, and can immediately see why. The man is drowning.

Replacing the camera in my pocket, and still smarting from the disgrace at Fanning Head, I volunteer to go down. Gleeson looks at me strangely but winches the strop back up. A moment later I'm descending towards the surface of the sea. A lot of memories came back at the rush. Winchmen are usually properly dressed in immersion clothing, and are always earthed via a discharge wire before they make contact, to disperse the likely build-up of static voltage. There is no time for this luxury here.

The discharging electric shock, quite literally, just precedes the shock of immersion. Sudden numbering cold envelops my body as I gasp for breath, while Mike, with marvellous precision flying, tows me across the swell towards the survivor. The desperate look on the man's face, his frantic thrashings and punctured life-jacket say it all. Our outstretched hands touch, grasp, and suddenly I have him in a fierce bearhug. There is no other way to secure him, and up we go.

Corporal Gleeson displays skill and strength in getting us both back into the cabin. Exhausted, I collapse on top of the survivor, then remember that there's someone else down there. The crewman looks at me anxiously as I don the winch strop once more, then grins and gives me an encouraging pat on the shoulder as he puts me down again.

This time a twist has developed in the winch wire and I spiral slowly during the descent. A mad Cinerama projection unfolds before my eyes. The burning outline of *Ardent*, her crew watching; *Yarmouth*; *Broadsword*, now close to us for air protection; Grantham Sound, the Falkland shore, then *Ardent* again.

I watch, stunned and chilled, until just above the surface when a new sight appears on the merry-go-round. Lying there quietly in the swell, arms outstretched and blood streaming downwind from a large cut in his forehead, the second survivor watches me with uncomprehending eyes. Bang! The static voltage discharges again and I'm in the water alongside him. I know that I am now too weak to lift him bodily, and think instead about slipping the strop and placing it around his body. I will have to take my chances in the interim. But instinct saves the day. At the top of each swell, the winch wire goes slack, sufficiently slack to allow me to get the winch hook into a small nylon becket on the front of his life jacket. It shouldn't work really, but it does, and together we are lifted up to the safety of the helicopter's cabin.

My jaw is now rattling with cold so Mike Crabtree orders the door closed and puts the cabin heaters on full blast. Agonizingly, slowly, sensation returns. I can now feel things with my fingers again and they touch – the camera still in my anorak pocket. It is ruined. We deliver our customers to *Canberra*, then Mike says, 'Well *done*, Doc. Bloody marvellous.' After Fanning Head I feel a lot better now, and we are all square.

We fly back to the scene. *Ardent* has now been abandoned because her main magazines are about to blow. We are ordered clear, so instead I winch down with the two special stretchers to *Yarmouth* which has now all the survivors on board. In the emergency sick bay that has been made out of the frigate's wardroom, the young Surgeon Lieutenant is in complete control, pointing out the seriously injured for priority of evacuation while calmly suturing two lacerated scalps. It is marvellous stuff and I am very proud of him. That pride is tinged with sadness, however, because *Ardent*'s medical officer, Surgeon Lieutenant Simon Ridout, was last seen floating in the sea having been blown over the side. He is missing, presumed dead.

The men of *Ardent* are winched up from *Yarmouth*'s flight deck into one of the stream of helicopters that has now arrived to help. We come alongside *Canberra*, and the remainder of the hollow-eyed and tired survivors transfer to the liner via her white passenger boats. Still damp from my immersion, I join them.

On board *Canberra* they have been very busy and, as dusk

falls, the Action Medical Organisation swings into top gear. Now, with the risk of air attack gone, the surgeons can work uninterrupted and they start on their long lists. A quick tour of the Bonito Club reveals my two survivors asleep but comfortable. Both have injuries of sufficient severity to require morphine. As I stare at the second survivor, he opens his eyes and looks at me again. His parched lips are moving. As I bend closer to hear the words, I remember that someone has given me a paper cup with a tot of rum in it. His whispered thanks mean a lot to me. With Peter Mayner's approval, I moisten his lips and tongue with a few drops of rum from my finger. Chief Enticknapp's face relaxes into a smile, and an instant later he is asleep once more.

Later, as I change in my small cabin, another message comes through. Simon Ridout has, miraculously, survived after all and is in *Broadsword*. The relief of that news is quickly forgotten with the next Command bombshell.

Canberra is to sail that night, away from San Carlos and her charges, away to the safety of South Georgia. Hurriedly, we assemble what kit we can man-pack, mainly surgical instruments and stores. There will be no cranes or helicopters to unload the freight chacons on the upper deck, so it is pointless taking No. 3 Troop ashore, or even the Band. *Canberra* still has a lot of work to do. Instead, Headquarters of Medical Squadron and the Plymouth SST are to get ashore as soon as possible to Red Beach. There (we think) we will meet No. 1 Troop from *Sir Lancelot*, and possibly also the Parachute Clearing Troop from *Norland*.

My wet clothing is still hanging up to dry in the cabin. I have no proper boots, only wellies. In the tearing rush to get down to the loading area on time, we all leave little things behind. At 0230 a Landing Craft Utility pulls alongside the gunport door. In pitch darkness we load stores, freight, baggage, weapons and personnel. Everything has happened so quickly that there is no time to take stock.

With the last metal bins and gas cylinders loaded, the LCU pulls away from *Canberra*'s tall side. The liner gets under way almost immediately, gathering speed as her pale and ghostly bulk disappears in the direction of Fanning Head. Under the sparkling and clear night sky our LCU chugs quietly past several darkened ships towards its destination. An hour later, at 0330, the ramp goes down and we struggle over the rocks in the darkness, towards the trackway laid by the Amphibious Beach Unit. The surgical stores, the cardboard replenishment boxes, and our bergans are all carried slowly and carefully up to the main entrance of the building. Complete blackout is enforced because of the very real risk of counter-attack from West Falkland. The Argy commander there will have had a grandstand view of events in Falkland Sound during D-Day and *should* be getting his act together for a riposte.

Entering the darkened building, lit only by a couple of Tilley lamps, I find that Malcolm and his boys have come ashore safely together with their kit. The PCT are also in residence, trying to tamp holes through the thick walls for the exhaust pipes of their small electrical generators.

0530 Too many people wandering about exploring and chattering. I tell everyone to get their sleeping mats out and their heads down. First light is at 1121 – and we have to 'stand to' in case of dawn attack. My military talents in organising fire positions and clearing patrols are about what you'd expect from a Naval obstetrician, even a Commando-trained one. Luckily, their Lordships understand this point and we have Lieutenant Fred Cook and WO2 Terry Moran to look after that side of the shop. A last look around and, exhausted, I fall asleep immediately.

Saturday, May 22

Dawn passes without incident. If the sky *had* blossomed with Argentinian parachutes, heralding the counter-attack from West Falkland, it would have been an interesting start to the day. The Marines of Medical Squadron are glad to be ashore in a real soldiering role, even if their job is a defensive one. The forefingers that sweat and itch around the trigger guards of the many machine guns are highly trained. Nonetheless, counter-attack must remain a serious threat if the Argy commander in Fox Bay is worth his salt. The Land Force is going to be utterly dependent on the logistic formations for its daily issue of bread and bullets. Even if the rumoured paratroop force is not called in to do the job, we face a tremendous and continuing threat from what remains of the Argentine Air Force.

First priorities, therefore, relate to preparing trenches outside, with adequate protection overhead. Stimulated by multiple episodes of heavy adrenalin release yesterday, the boys need no encouragement to dig for their lives. The wet peat blocks are cut from the rocky soil all around the building, then stacked to make walls reinforced by some of the bigger stones. Human ingenuity appears unlimited when associated with survival. One shelter has a right-angled turn in the entrance porch while another, built by some SST personnel, looks clearly suited for the nuclear age.

With somewhere to run out to when the air raid warnings are given, the boys now turn to the business of setting up shop inside the building. The Ajax Bay complex is shaped like a large 'T', the spine running north to south and longer in length than the cross bar, which in turn is wider. At the base of the 'T' there appears to have been an open slaughterhouse, because an overhead rail system begins here to carry the mutton carcasses on into the chilling-down and storage areas. There are windows here, too, or the remains of them, and the floor is ankle deep in rusting rubbish and tie-on meat labels.

The remainder of the areas in the building are cold, airless and devoid of light. Each major sub-division contains refrigeration plant along one wall, a complex network of large-calibre pipes and associated pumping machinery. The walls and floors are dusty and dirty but, thankfully, the rooms seem to be dry and vermin-free. Lighting is an immediate problem because 1 Troop's electric generator has not taken kindly to repeated immersion in South Atlantic spray. For a while I consider the merits of moving into the slaughterhouse area, to be sure of enough operating light at least between dawn and dusk, but two events then solve this problem. Workshop Squadron lend us a 6kVA generator which begins to perform faultlessly, then 45 Commando annex most of the area as their Quartermaster's supply depot. We stay where we are, a lucky break in the light of what is to happen later.

Pressure is also building to put some kind of surgical presence on board one of the ships at anchor in San Carlos Water. Eventually we compromise and I send Tim Riley, a Commando-trained resuscitation officer, to *Intrepid*, as leader of a small team which we call SST2 Alpha. They are almost totally frustrated by the lack of space or suitable facilities on board. Once again, common sense has lost out to theory.

Back on shore, things are much better. With a bit of ingenuity in stacking boxes and rigging blanket screens, we soon set up a Command Post as well as a casualty flow system. In through the main door, triage to sort out priorities and documentation, resuscitation to get the serious injured fit for operation, and then the two theatres themselves. The flow loops back on itself then, out into the post-operative area and high-and-low dependency 'wards'.

The theatres have been chosen as such because the roof has been heavily strengthened there. The PCT are soon in business with two operating tables rigged and lit, surrounded by the stores boxes. They are certainly an interesting lot, individuals for the most part, of widely differing temperaments and attitudes, all immensely enthusiastic about the Airborne aspects of war.

The CO of the Commando Logistics Regiment has not yet been allowed ashore by Brigade, so his daily 'O' Group is held instead on the LSL *Sir Galahad*. With the weather deteriorating, our ride out to the ship is a rollercoaster nightmare in the small rigid raider that is sent to collect us. Conditions worsen, so I'm glad later on when we are marooned on board for the night. There is the chance instead for a glass of beer with some of the other Squadron Commanders, as well as the pilots who have yet to hear how Ken Francis and his crewman died on D-Day.

My second night's sleep in the Falklands is on a spare mattress, but without a sleeping bag, or 'green slug' to zip into, things don't seem quite the same.

Sunday, May 23

I return ashore with Lieutenant Colonel Hellberg. As wind and weather have abated we are only slightly wet when reaching land again.

A quick brief to the lads about how the battle is going, then a Sea King arrives as our daily dedicated casevac aircraft. We address ourselves to the problem of whether or not to paint Red Crosses on the roof of the building. The decision turns on the fact that Ajax Bay is so confined and the area available for open storage so limited that we cannot honestly separate ourselves from the combat supplies. There is also a sneaky feeling about an enemy actually using the Red Cross as a morale-smashing aiming mark. We note that Argentina is not in fact a signatory of the Geneva Convention.

Relationships between the various groups attached to Medical Squadron seem to be unpredictable, and after a couple of little niggling incidents I decide to face up to the problem. Everyone is ordered to fall in outside. Standing on a large wooden container with the various sub-unit leaders, I introduce each one to the assembled groups. And groups are what they remain in. The paras stand together in a little huddle, the marines separate from them, and the naval types hang back on their own. As I half expect, the introductions bring little cheers and hisses from rival factions, so I get really mad and let them have both barrels. We *have* to work together because there are 5,000 potential customers out there who don't care who looks after them, just as long as they get fixed up properly. The PCT looked surprised, my Squadron look a bit hurt, and the SST appear confused. But the message sinks in. Later on I notice that they have stopped wearing their different berets and have taken to talking to each other instead. We are beginning to become a team.

A little later we receive a message from Log HQ down on the beach. 3 Para have sustained casualties, eight men, perhaps ten. A helicopter is inbound. WO2 'Phred' New-bound and WO2 Fritz Sterba, the two PCT senior theatre technicians, break out some first-line stores in readiness. There is a delay, too long a delay knowing 3 Para's rough position just north of Port San Carlos, so I walk down to HQ again. For some reason the whole lot have been flown to *Intrepid*! We flash the Sea King up in a hurry and land on the LPD's empty deck.

Inside the main dining hall there is organized chaos. All our direct predictions have come true. *Intrepid* is nowhere near suitable as a prime casualty-handling facility. The SST2 Alpha boys are working flat out to get drips going and blood transfusions set up. A number of longish-haired gentlemen in military clothing – patrol medics from the SAS – are also helping. Tim Riley is both concise and despairing in his brief. Two men have penetrating head wounds and look unlikely survival prospects. I take ashore the three worst injured and return later for the rest while Tim and his men clear up. Later, Nick Morgan and Andy Yates operate on one of the few wounded who is fit enough to be moved up a ladder to the wardroom.

Ashore, Bill McGregor and Phil Shouler get on with the remainder of the injured. Later on, Bill removes a bullet from the brain of one of the 'hopeless' cases, and George Rudge puts to work his skills as a jaw surgeon by tidying up the other's head wound beautifully. Throughout this period air raids are developing with increasing frequency and, for the first time, surgeons, anaesthetists and theatre staff face the tremendous strain of divided loyalties. Should a man obey instincts of self-preservation and run for his slit trench when the six whistle blasts are blown? Or should he stay at his post, by the operating table? The traditions persist and they ignore the whistles.

During one attack I note that the figures on the skyline around us have dropped out of sight and am still unsure why when a Mirage flies over the distant Sussex Ridge. Several of us stand slack-jawed as a Rapier sprints upwards and takes it in the tailpipe. Our cheers are loud and long, later confirmed on the radio that five out of six Daggers (the Israeli version of the Mirage which the Argentinians fly) have been splashed.

But not without cost to the Royal Navy. Late in the afternoon, HMS *Antelope* steams into the anchorage, well away from the other ships. She has a hole in her starboard side and the top of her mast leans over at a drunken angle, actually struck by a low flying A-4. The Type 21 anchors to begin the process of defusing and removing the unexploded bomb lodged deep in her hull. On the far side of San Carlos Water HMS *Argonaut* is doing much the same. Although out of battle temporarily, they lie under the protective steel umbrella of both fleet and shore anti-aircraft missiles.

Because we are busy I have to miss the daily 'O' Group, so Peter Lansley attends instead.

Suddenly, a heavy explosion rattles the walls. In the dusk we can see that a bomb has exploded in HMS *Antelope*. The ship's Lynx helicopter arrives with the colleague of the missing bomb disposal expert. A flying hatch cover has all but severed WO2 Phillips' left arm, and Phil Shouler does a neat amputation in the PCT theatre. More inter-service rivalry blown away in the wind. Bill McGregor watches quietly, assessing and judging, and constantly popping out to see what is happening in triage. I realize how lucky we are to have Bill with us. He is a calming and encouraging influence of huge experience, and is no mean wielder of the knife himself. We take six casualties in all.

That night we introduce the PCT to an old Naval custom – that of issuing a tot of rum to those involved in 'arduous duty'. Our limited stocks will suffice for two issues only. This new custom, and the tots themselves, go down extremely well.

Outside, the fire takes hold of *Antelope* and gradually, like some dreaful cancer eating into the heart of the ship, the flames spread from midships right along the hull. She burns down towards the waterline and, in a shower of sparks, the aft Seacat launcher explodes. The lads watch silently in the darkness by the main door. Seeing a ship die like this is agony for anyone who has ever loved the Navy and its way of life. It's all bad, bad news.

Monday, May 24

Antelope is still on fire, but is glowing rather than burning. As first light turns to dawn we can see that her main feature now is a huge grey plume of smoke drifting and climbing slowly to the south. All the patients from last night are well, especially the two lads with head injuries whom we had labelled as 'hopeless' in the first instance! They can both sit up, open their eyes, and swallow liquids. One can even give his name and number which is *tremendous*.

I set off to *Intrepid*, to try and find *Uganda*'s whereabouts as well as repossess the surgical team led by Tim Riley. A series of air raids come in under a blue, blue sky. In the ship's wardroom we cower on the floor as Captain Peter Dingeman's metallic tannoy voice calls the strikes, ending with the urgent command: 'TAKE COVER - TAKE COVER!' I'm very conscious of not having any anti-flash gear to put on, but the SAS and SBS men in the corner just sit quietly, ignoring all the fuss and reading their newspapers. The machine guns chatter away, reverberating throughout the ship, echoed by the slower and heavier thuds of the Bofors.

Once again, General Lami Dozo's boys have done their stuff and delivered the loads on target, but the bombs are duff. Two UXBs in one ship, one in another. The crews are evacuated to Ajax Bay, and *Antelope* sinks in the middle of all this, her brave back finally broken by the smouldering fire. The cold sea rushes in, and a towering pillar of steam and smoke rises to the sky above the still-surfaced bow and stern sections. These settle slowly beneath the surface too, until the only trace left floating is an emergency life raft, still tied to her hull beneath, its Day-Glo canopy contrasting starkly with the grey and fuel-slicked water all around.

Ashore, I find that the boys have seen the whole attack. One of the Skyhawks turned towards them after releasing its bombs. It screamed over the roof of our building so low, and

68

banked over so sharply, that they could see the pilot's white helmet. Brave as he is, I fervently hope that this chap has been caught by the Sea Harriers on the way home. There is a good reason for my apparent callousness. If that jet was carrying cameras in its nose then Ajax Bay's status will alter. Overnight we will move right to the top of the Fuerza Aerea Argentina's hit list.

My chums from *Sir Galahad* are somewhat taken aback by the primitive conditions in which we are working. Everything seems so unreal to them after the relative physical comforts enjoyed in their floating grey hotel. For my part I would much rather take my chances ashore but they disagree, particularly Les Short, a REME major who commands Workshop Squadron. With a soldier's sixth sense, he had ordered all his men out of the building into permanent accommodation out on the ground. He tells some tremendous and amusing stories about life afloat during the air attacks.

Lieutenant Commander Gervase Coryton, a Fleet Air Arm Gazelle pilot on exchange with the Royal Marines, was actually on board for once during an air attack and rushed up to the bridge to get a better look. Grabbing a pair of binoculars he stood out on the starboard bridge wing, focused the instrument and announced: 'Ah, here comes one. A-4 I think . . .' There was a crash as the pilot leapt backwards into the wheelhouse, a strangled cry of 'Bloody *hell*' and a huge bang as a 30mm cannon shell passed through the upperworks where he'd been standing. After that Gervase stayed airborne whenever he could.

Later on, the ship's company and embarked force were listening intently to the broadcast announcements of developing attacks, playing the serious game of rushing over to the side away from the attack in order to minimize the human cost of a cannon strike. *Sir Galahad*, on these occasions, would rock from side to side with the sudden shift of weight. The Second Officer came on main broadcast during one afternoon air raid: 'Two high-speed hostiles to the east, and closing . . . *and* another pair to the south west, also approaching fast. Gentlemen – take your pick!'

Tuesday, May 25

A famous Argentinian holiday. Everyone hopes secretly that their carrier – the *Vientecinquo de Mayo* – will come out and fight, although we understand the Argy Navy's reluctance. The *General Belgrano*'s loss must have cooled a few of the more volcanic hotheads, including Admiral Anaya who is supposed to have told Galtieri that taking and keeping the Falklands would be a doddle. Perhaps, we tell ourselves hopefully, Sandy Woodward has a master plan up his sleeve for today, and the first part of the Fleet Air Arm ditty will come true:

> Don't cry for me Argentina
> The truth is we will defeat you
> And with our Sea Harrier
> We'll zap your carrier . . .

But there are other, more pressing, problems. At last we have a Sea King to ourselves *and* a definite booking for SS *Uganda*. There are immense problems contacting the converted liner, because her Red Cross Hospital Ship status means that all transmissions to her are 'in clear' and uncoded. We have to ask London to ask her to be in the right place a day later! I can see that we are going to have problems.

The promised Sea King arrives from *Intrepid* at first light and the crewman asks *me* where *Uganda* is! I send them all back to their Mother to find out. That aircraft goes unserviceable, so Lieutenant John Miller turns up in another Sea King. No problems there. John is an old and sensible friend from Norway and Salisbury Plain days. He lifts at 1250 with five stretchers, four sitting casualties and Bill McGregor acting as escort/liaison.

I sense that we are beginning a tremendous period in our lives. By the accidents of happenstance and fate we have, pooled together, in Ajax Bay, a team of medical officers and men who are determined, tough and capable. Our customers are very fit too, and seem able to absorb injuries that would kill lesser men. Bill's request to go as the first escort to *Uganda* is typical. He has now assessed Phil Shouler as capable of covering a serious emergency, and is anxious to establish exactly what *Uganda* can do. Although not actually in command of the PCT – that responsibility devolves on Peter Lansley – he is certainly in command of Ajax Bay's surgical standards. From what I have seen so far his background of war experience in the Middle East and Northern Ireland has produced the true battle surgeon – a man who is quick to decide priorities, determined in attacking the heart of the operative problem, and generous in his encouragement of subordinates.

Away from the table he is a gentle, rather shy man who speaks with a quiet Scots burr. While the others play cards, Bill reads and smokes. Tiredness never seems to affect his attitude, either to me or to the patients. We are both lucky to have him around.

Charles Batty, the second cutter in the PCT is different altogether. A big, strong and cheerful fellow, he has had some trouble with one of the professional examinations along the surgical road. Frankly, I'm surprised at this, because although he is slower than Bill, his skill with the knife is definitely there. Perhaps he holds opinions too strongly in the eyes of the examiners – that must certainly apply in the case of Malcolm Jowitt, the RAMC Major who is Bill McGregor's anaesthetist. A thin, blue-eyed man with a short haircut and strong jawline, Malcolm is obviously a determined individual. He has been at the base of the anaesthetic pyramid for some time, but his style and performance complement Bill's wonderfully, even though their personalities are completely different.

The other anaesthetist is Dick Knight, a cheerful fellow with an impish sense of humour and a quick, darting mind. Every morning he checks on the welfare of *Elk*, because the P&O freighter's captain is godfather to one of his children. Like Bill McGregor, he is a welcome source of practical consultant-level advice to his younger and less experienced anaesthetic colleagues.

An hour and a half later the Sea King returns. *Uganda* is sitting in her 'Red Cross Box' about 50 miles north of us. John Miller takes another load, and returns two hours later with Bill and some welcome blankets and sheets. The medical and nursing staff on *Uganda* have apparently been shocked to see our filthy, exhausted patients with their bandaged wounds unsutured. No one has been telling them the big picture about the war, although they have seen some Mirages and a flight of bombed-up Skyhawks around. Suddenly they have realized exactly where they are – right near the front line.

Our overnight guests depart. Outside, the simple slit trenches are being further reinforced. Overhead cover is now very much the in thing, and several elaborate roof constructions involving old doors, sandbags and thick clods of peat appear.

Throughout the day the air raid warnings also continue. The information leading to these alerts comes from varied sources and are not always reliable. Still, the bowels turn to ice-water when six short whistle blasts are blown, or *Intrepid*'s mournful whistle echoes around the bay. Typically, the only serious air raid that we are involved in is preceded by – nothing! A pair of W4s comes screeching in from the south and one of the Argentinians discovers that a Rapier missile has mated with his port wing. He ejects just in time because his parachute canopy is only in the air for a few seconds. A landing craft picks him up, then takes him to *Fearless* where the PMO gives him morphia and sends him to us.

I can't help feeling sorry for Teniente Primero (1st Lt) Ricardo Lucero. He is a small, dark, frightened man with large, fleshy earlobes whose left kneecap is about four inches away from its customary position. His flying suit has been cut off on *Fearless*, but he still has his orange silk squadron scarf tucked around his neck. We try and tell him through Corporal Jim Pearson, our part-time interpreter, that his knee requires an operation and that he will wake up with his leg in a plaster cylinder. The worry lines on his face remain however, until Malcolm Jowitt slides some of his favourite Kefamine and diazepam cocktail into an arm vein and the enemy pilot relaxes into sleep. Charles Batty then does a careful and effective manipulation of the fractured knee, restoring the designs of nature.

We hear a report on the radio about Skyhawks and Mirages passing to the south but think no more of it until, suddenly – disaster. HMS *Coventry* has been sunk and, it is rumoured, the *Atlantic Conveyor* too. I know from the daily logistic briefings that the big container ship has a lot of our specialist resupply items on board, including hundreds of accommodation tents. The heavy-lift Chinooks were also being ferried on deck. Helicopter hours are getting fewer and more precious as the Naval pilots flog their airframes and engines to the point of collapse, so there is much cause for gloom.

Then, the sound of clattering rotor blades and the arrival of a load of injured *Coventry* survivors. Soaked and burnt, they are shivering with cold and pain. Eight living and one dead – the Chinese second laundryman. Their skin damage has been caused by flash burns as the bombs went off below the Operations Room. It is interesting to note just how well the anti-flash hood and gloves have defended the face and hands of those who were wearing them. We cover their burns with Flamazine, a thick white cream which is both pain-killing and antiseptic, then lay them on *Uganda*'s cool sheets, their stretchers down at floor level.

One of the young stokers, his skinned hands in plastic bags, eyes the sleeping Ricardo Lucero aggressively. The fire that burned his hands now burns in his soul and he cannot understand our friendliness towards this colleague of the men who killed his ship.

Then the morphine takes hold, and like the rest of the white-faced marionettes from *Sheffield*'s once proud sister ship, the young stoker falls asleep.

Wednesday, May 26

Another lovely day – curses! Fred Cook comes in for some stick about his pronouncements on Falklands weather. He is always maintaining from his experience down here with Naval Party 8901 that no two days are the same, and that blue skies in winter are almost unheard of.

Last night's rumours are true but there are 450 survivors. A couple of sporadic air raid warnings come in the early afternoon but, really, things are ominously quiet. Charles Laurence of the *Telegraph* and Kim Sabido from Independent Radio News come to interview Ricardo. The pilot seems much chirpier, and gabbles away in Spanish, the worry lines on his face now gone. Like any other soldier who has done his duty and survived, he is concerned about his wife and family in Cordoba. I arrange for him to write a Red Cross letter.

The Fleet Diving Team also arrive to stay with us, led by an irrepressible character named Bernie Bruen. His affection for proper naval rum and his carefully cased fiddle are combined with semi-professional abilities as a raconteur, but disguise his true nature. He is a hard man with a deep determination and knowledge of bombs, mines and illegal explosive devices. The Team will have a crack at *Sir Lancelot*'s bomb tomorrow. After *Antelope*, no one envies them one little bit.

There is time to look around the area in greater detail. Piled up outside the front of our dressing station are the 1 Troop chacons from *Sir Galahad*. The narrow road runs for approximately 100 metres, from east to west and down the slight slope to the beach. Parallel with the spine of the 'T'-shaped main building is a second and smaller construction which is now being used as a storehouse, distribution centre and field Records Office. The latter outfit is under the command of Captain Roy Hancock, a genial and cheerful Royal Marines officer who gets on famously with us and is always a welcome visitor to the Command Post. This close relationship is to prove priceless in terms of the speed and accuracy with which casualty information is transmitted back to England.

The road ends just above the beach, continuing on special metal trackway down to the left, past the water point and the tents of the Amphibious Beach Unit. Colour Sergeant McDowell is our 'Mr Fixit' here and the source of much help to the medics. The rather grubby beach then runs round to the edge of the bay where rubbish is stacked and burned when conditions permit.

There are tents here too, and the residents find and adopt a lost penguin whose glistening feathers have been soiled by the fuel oil that now slicks San Carlos Water. 'Marine Galtieri' waddles around cheerfully and develops a taste for compo biscuit mixed with a little whisky. The bird is an amusing distraction and an outlet for the men's affection, a welcome change from the harsher realities of war.

Where the road peters out to the right, a large sandbag sangar has been built, with two separate compartments. In one the Duty Officer and his signaller hold court. The other houses the Combat Supplies Cell of Ordnance Squadron whose job it is to identify the whereabouts of stores demanded by the units and co-ordinate their delivery, by whatever means available, up to the front. Inside the main Log CP, Captain Paddy George, Regimental Adjutant, is usually to be found hunched over the paraffin stove, trying to make sense of the information passed over the radio. We tease each other gently, aware of the value of humour under these conditions. My favourite response to the latest of his daily, multiple crises is to ask: 'Shall I make out a list?'

The line catches on and raises a laugh every time. He and the Operations Officer, Captain Colin Healey, have the near-impossible job of trying to satisfy everyone's requirements in this new experience of war. At least they are keeping the heat off Ivar Hellberg.

The CO lives in the back of his long-wheelbase Land Rover, parked between the two buildings. He is a shy, smiling figure and an expert mountaineer and skier. Even when the logistic pressures are highest with yet more tasks imposed on his small and inadequate number of troops, Ivar H. is never glum. His favourite mental escape route lies in the planning of a 1983 re-enactment of the Rjukan 'Heavy Water' raid, by a group know much more widely, thanks to Hollywood and Kirk Douglas, as the Heroes of Telemark. He keeps suggesting that I should accompany him as exped. medical officer, and I keep reminding him that, after one descent from the tailgate of a Hercules, only fools jump out of perfectly serviceable aeroplanes.

Terry Knott also comes into his own here. Long and lean, he wears a canvas belt around his waist which contains extra magazines of SLR amunition and grenades. He is in effect the 'gauleiter' of Ajax Bay, responsible for the defence of the logistic area as well as the welfare of any prisoners. His flashing smile hides a tremendous determination as a professional soldier, and the same instincts and courage which accompanied him down a helicopter rope into a mountain cave above Aden. He still carries the pistol he used that day in winning the Military Cross. The marines on the ground can sense his natural abilities as a tough leader, and a soldier capable of maintaining high wartime personal standards. For my part I'm very glad to have Terry around to look after our defence.

Mail! A letter arrives from Susie, full of news, but long delayed. All around the area men read and re-read their messages from home. If the boys driving the Michigan tractors and Eager Beaver fork-lifts up and down the trackway with logistic stores are key features of the war at present, then mail is the single most important factor affecting morale. Hope it keeps coming.

Food is much less of a worry. The main galley has now been opened in a much-tidied slaughterhouse area. The drainage gullies that used to run with sheep blood, and then became choked with rusting debris for over twenty years, now carry away the dirty hot water of a facility feeding nearly 200 men. The chefs are an extrovert, hard-working bunch who take a pride in being chefs – *never* 'cooks'.

Smoking and spitting in one corner of the galley area is our Field Immersion Water Heater. This £50 device was 'loaned' to us on trial by some American Army medics in Germany. It was spotted there by my predecessor in Medical Squadron,

Surgeon Commander Charles Evans. We have tried very trick in the book to get six more, but have been baulked at each turn. There is a disease that affects many government purchasing agencies called the 'not-invented-here' syndrome. Our simple, cheap and reliable water heater uses ordinary petrol and can even melt packed snow. Clamped to the side of an ordinary dustbin, a tap drips petrol on to a baffle plate above a doughnut-shaped steel burning chamber. The water or snow surrounding and cooling this chamber then gets hot in the process.

Unfortunately, too much petrol can result in an explosion which lifts the exhaust stack up and away, sometimes as much as twenty yards. As a result the American nickname for it is 'kitchen-mortar', but ours is merely old, hard-worked and very blackened. Without the 'African Queen' we would be lost. Chief Petty Officers Scouse Davis and John Smith each keep a paternal and quartermasterly eye on the heater as they drain it frequently to fill the communal tea urns.

That night sees the last enactment of an important ritual. Jack, the pharmacy dispenser in *Canberra*, gave Bryn Dobbs a large bag of salted peanuts as a going-ashore present. Each night since we have solemnly celebrated another day survived by dipping into the bag for a handful. Someone jokes about out luck running out along with the peanuts. There is nervous laughter as the torches are flicked off.

Thursday, May 27

The young chefs have really got things sorted out now and produce a hot breakfast at 0800 for the night shift, three hours before dawn. Breakfast is invariably the same – tinned sausage, baked beans and a 'wet' of tea or coffee, but it is hot and very welcome for that. This morning I surface, for once, in time to try it out.

A Sea King arrives for *Uganda*, and can manage just one round trip with the *Coventry* survivors before being diverted to another task. The morning is spent at Brigade HQ and with various heavies discussing the details of medical support forward when the breakout from the San Carlos bridgehead is ordered. We evolve, I think, a reasonable plan. The suggested use of HMS *Intrepid* and her large tank deck as a floating hospital is less than satisfactory, but we'll do our very best if ordered to go ahead. It's certainly a more viable alternative than the use of her wardroom which is so far from the flight deck.

Back at Ajax Bay I discuss these plans with Phil Shouler, the leader of the Naval SST. He is a chubby-faced Senior Registrar back home in Plymouth but has considerable surgical experience, both in hospitals and at sea. We tease him about the lack of Mars bars affecting his survival prospects, but he is very good-natured and fails to rise to the bait. Andy Yates, his anaesthetist, is still a deep bronzed colour from excessive sun worship off Ascension. He seems quite capable, but then the Naval team has not had much to do so far. Nick Morgan, the junior surgeon, still looks as though he's losing weight, no mean achievement for a man built like a racing greyhound. He is a former Commando MO and has just started surgical training.

Outside the building, sporadic air raid warnings are blown on the whistle now secured to the door. Men are getting more used to this phenomenon and now tend to watch others on

78

the skyline surrounding them as well as the helicopters. As long as the 'paraffin parrots' keep flying in to pick up supplies or land passengers, we can be sure that enemy aircraft are reasonably far away. When they suddenly lift off and dive into a nearby gulley for shelter, then it's time for tin hats.

I've never found a steel helmet to fit my size 7¾ head, so put my trust in the magical, shrapnel-deflecting powers of the Commando green beret instead!

1900 Supper, in the main galley. The usual, but nonetheless excellent, chicken curry. Tonight's choice lies in rice or mashed potatoes!

1945 Air Raid Warning Red. The galley empties quickly. The sun is sinking low in a clear sky as I walk round to the main entrance. Inside the building I know that Bill McGregor and Charles Batty are operating on two Argentinian patients. Phil and his team are off watch. A loud 'kerrump' from the other side of San Carlos Water heralds an air attack on Brigade HQ in San Carlos Settlement. The large grey mushroom cloud develops vertically in the still air as I watch, wondering if I should get some staff ready to send over there, to help with the inevitable casualties.

Suddenly there comes the hoarse cry of 'TAKE COVER!' and HMS *Plymouth*, lying close to Red Beach, starts blazing away with Bofors and machine guns at a target out of sight behind the main building. Adrenalin flows and I sprint to the nearest sangar, diving into it as a loud 'whoomph' blends into the roar of a jet passing low overhead. My arrival in the sangar has been preceded by Marines John Nelson and Nutsy Naughton, and we are now all three covered with a thick layer of dust, small stones and dirt.

Poking my head out of the sanger I see a San Carlos mushroom cloud again, only this time in close-up, emerging from the main galley area. Instinct takes over. The Marines scramble out after me and go for stretchers, while I race into the building for morphine. Threading through the accommodation passages at the back we emerge into Dante's Inferno. The main galley is shattered and broken, and in 45 Commando's storage area, ammunition is starting to explode.

Even more strangely, there are men everywhere. From

their sangars and foxholes all around the building they have emerged to help their mates and fight the fire. A case of 105mm anti-tank ammunition explodes with such a loud bang that I fear for the health of my Sergeant Major, who I know is in there somewhere. Suddenly Terry Morgan emerges, eyes out on organ stops, his face such a picture that I shout with laughter and relief. It serves him right. He shared a sangar with Fleet Chief Bryn Dobbs and could only laugh hysterically at the poor man after the latter's scalp had been opened up by a piece of shrapnel or stone fragment.

Now our own injured are coming in. Young Danny Mudge, his forearm shredded; A Royal Marines chef named Callan with a big steel bomb splinter through his belly; two other young marines from Logistics, Burnett and Watt, both badly mangled. The system swings into gear, and within minutes the worst cases are on the tables.

Bill McGregor again, deep in tiger country beneath Callan's liver, trying to patch a hole in the inferior vena cava and a tear into the duodenum . . . Malcolm Jowett pouring blood and skill in equal measures into the same patient. The Naval team turn to at the rush and start work on Marine Mudge.

Then the RAF Flight Lieutenant, a bomb disposal expert, who is lodging with us, quietly comes up to me. 'Excuse me, sir, will you come and look at this, please?' He takes me to one of the accommodation spaces, two walls away from the PCT theatre. The lights are out, but the strong beam of his torch picks out an incredible sight. Embedded in the grey metal pipework of the refrigeration machinery at the far end of the room is a greenish metal cylinder. From one end, a tangled skein of nylon webbing leads to what looks like a parachute draped though a neat hole in the wall.

When Alan Swann tells me that this is a French 400kg high-explosive bomb, my first instinct is to turn and run. He grins at my evident discomfort, and then tells me of a *second* device lying in the ceiling above our heads!

There are obviously some big decisions to take now, and we discuss the options. With his natural caution and understandable desire to cut all risks to the minimum, Alan wants the building evacuated – prisoners, patients, surgical teams – the lot. My instinct says that we should stay if possible, because the surrounding ground is terrible and we certainly won't get a tented facility erected that will be anywhere near as good as this, bombs or no bombs.

Luckily, Ivar Hellberg then joins us and listens in on the conversation. As my direct boss, he makes up his mind quickly, and his decision echoes my instincts. Only the immediate area is to be evacuated and placed out of bounds. The ceiling is to be shored up beneath the second bomb, and the intervening walls are to be reinforced, probably with sandbags, by the naval diving team.

To compound our anxiety, Flt Lt Swann then produces a chart prepared by Engins Matra showing the various types of fuse which can be fitted to their bombs. The labelling of these diagrams is in French, so Captain Mike von Bertele of the PCT lends his linguistic skills. One of these fuses is capable of a 33-hour delay! Again, instinct sways the decision. I think it unlikely, if the first bomb in the stick has had an impact fuse which detonated successfully, that the remainder should be fitted with timers. I feel that the Argentinian armourers back in Rio Gallegos will have kept things simple, and fortunately Ivar H. agrees. We will persist with our plan, but we will also do our very best to find somewhere to move to in the morning.

Malcolm Hazell, the Troop OC, leaves at once by boat to travel across San Carlos Water and look for alternative sites. I find Brigadier Julian Thompson standing in Reception surveying the scene quietly. He is grim-faced and obviously moved by the suffering being endured by the wounded. His tired eyes bore into mine as he takes his leave: 'Well done, all of you. If there's anything you want, Rick, just ask for it.' I ask for *Uganda*, close in, first thing tomorrow morning, and then he is gone, with his key staff officers, to continue planning and fighting the war.

Back in the main theatres, the surgical teams have triumphed once more and the 100% track record is intact. It is definitely 'tot' time again and the issue goes out – rum for the Navy, whisky for the Army. I discuss some of the news with Phil Shouler and Peter Lansley, as respective bosses of the SST and PCT. Bill and a few of the others listen in. We are to shrink into 50% of our previous space, converting the current operating theatres into storage and accommodation areas.

I do not mention the possibility of time fuses to them, nor the precautions that we are taking. Ammunition continues to explode 50 metres and four walls away from us, shaking everything and everyone with the concussion of the shock waves.

To my utter astonishment, Chief Davies then appears from the passageway at the back that leads down into the galley area. On his back is a rather battered and dusty-looking African Queen. He has taken something of a risk by collecting the water heater from the scene of devastation, so close to the exploding ammunition, but he's also having trouble keeping the tea urns topped up. A small group of anxious dependants gather round as he lovingly assembles the components outside.

An hour later the brew is as good as ever, with our trusty, reliable and useful friend back in business despite attempted Argentinian alterations. An elderly Phoenix, but a tough one – when will there be another such as this? I mention my problem again to Ivar Hellberg, and a gleam appears in the CO's eye. The plot for an African Queen replacement thickens, but he won't tell me what new ingredients he's going to add to the long-running saga!

Ricardo Lucero has been tremendous. The boys equipped him with a tin helmet and laid his stretcher on the floor during the attack. Now in full possession of his faculties, he must have known exactly what was going on. One of the Naval Medical Assistants tells me, over his tot, that when the Argentinian pilot saw the smashed and injured bodies coming in beside him, he burst into tears. Motioning the MA towards him, he took the blankets from his own naked body and indicated through his tears, that they should be used for the wounded.

A little later, I certify two men dead. Their corpses are partially burned, and one has also been badly torn up by blast. There are three more bodies outside at the back for the morning, to be picked up when or if the ammunition fires die down.

The night ends on a high note when I discuss the air attack with another of my marines. I'm still a bit puzzled by the roar that followed immediately after the explosion in the main galley area, and ask him if the Skyhawks were low.

'*Low*, boss?' comes the incredulous reply. 'Bloody 'ell, if the bastards had their bleeding wheels down, they'd have *landed*!'

The day dawns again, this time (thankfully) shrouded by fog and mist. We have all survived, and even Marine Callan is doing well. Out at the back, ammunition continues to cook off in a rather desultory way. There are two immediate priorities. The first is to get last night's customers to *Uganda* and, second, find out if there is anywhere else we can move to. Malcolm Hazell has completed a hair-raising trip through thick fog to Port San Carlos to recce the bunkhouse and sheep-shearing sheds as a medical facility, but his report is not encouraging.

Charlie the Chinook helps us with the first problem. With Mike von B. as escort, it flogs all the way out to *Uganda* which has not received our flash priority message! The pilot does a super job of landing athwartships, with only inches between the big helicopter's wheels and the heaving deck edge.

We also make an attempt to set up a tented facility on the far side of our clearing, but the ground is too rough and wet and, despite our Norway-proven storm lashings, the wind blows down one of the tents. Later, the down draught of the Chinook's huge rotor blades complete the destruction job, so we abandon the idea and let the main galley have the tents instead.

The expected assault on Goose Green has gone in. We were a bit surprised in last night's confusion to hear 2 Para's position given out on the BBC World Service as being 5km north of Darwin. I hope the Argies haven't taken the hint and reinforced with the air-mobile element of their reserves in Port Stanley. *We* have reinforced Steve Hughes with another MO, Captain Rory Waggon RAMC, and two NCOs from the PCT.

The Fleet Team blow a UXB down on the beach. The ceiling shakes and the whole building rattles although we are over 150 metres away. A huge crater appears in the sand and

Bernie's No 2, Chief Trotter, returns with a mega-grin across his face. Those boys love blowing things up as well as defusing them.

There are also some amusing tales emerging from last night's raid. A Staff Sergeant of Ordnance Squadron was actually standing naked in a washing up bowl, having what Royal Marines call a 'bird bath', when the A4s flashed over. A few seconds later he was seen, still naked and soapy, with his helmet on and shouting, 'Where's my towel?'

Equally funny was the reaction of two unfortunates down in the area where a small stream meets the beach. By common usage this has become a public toilet, flushed twice a day by the incoming tide. After the first bomb explosion there had been sympathetic detonation of an adjacent stack of mortar ammunition. As chunks of metal began whizzing in their direction they had no option but to get down flat, in the cover of dead ground. They may not smell nice, but at least they are survivors!

Les Short, now ashore, witnessed the whole thing from *Sir Galahad*. Two Skyhawks ran in low and dropped, he thinks, eight parachute-retarded bombs. At least four went off. As the aircraft climbed away to the north one was taken by Rapier, the other was later splashed by the CAP Sea Harriers. As we walk up the little road together I notice that there is now a hole in the front of our building, about five metres up and to the left of the main entrance. It looks like a rocket strike, because there is also a shallow crater about two metres long and ankle deep, lined up opposite the hole and on the far side of the roadway. The crater is freshly made, perhaps by an exploding rocket. If so, we've been quite lucky. The crater marks the spot where I was standing, about five metres from the sangar that I dived into.

Meanwhile there are other things to worry about, and more dramatic news. 2 Para have seized Darwin and are now positioned outside Goose Green. It is a tremendous feat of arms but has cost them dearly because their irrepressible Commanding Officer, 'H' Jones, has been killed in the run-up to the final assault.

Throughout the afternoon, helicopters arrive and unload wounded human cargo. Later, we tot up the numbers; nearly

80 casualties have been processed through the dressing station, with 47 actually operated on under general anaesthetic. We are now more than a dressing station – rather a field hospital, but without the appropriate scales of equipment!

In the confusion of pale, grimy faces and bleeding bodies two names stand out. First, Sergeant Belcher. A Royal Marines air gunner, he and his pilot were en route to pick up H in their Scout helicopter when it was attacked by a pair of Pucaras. The Argentinian twin turboprops are highly manoeuverable and heavily armed. After a desperate fight, the Scout crashed, somehow throwing Sergeant Belcher clear of the wreckage. Sitting up, he gave himself some morphia and tried to stem the lifeblood flowing from his legs. Another Scout picked *him* up and raced him to Ajax Bay. What a terrible mess. A 20mm cannon shell has pulverized his right leg and, almost as an encore, a machine gun bullet has traversed his left lower leg and ankle. The doctors in Resus stop the bleeding, pour fresh O neg into his depleted circulation – and then the surgeons amputate his right leg – mid-thigh. Then I discover the name of his pilot, and a chill feeling envelops me. Lieutenant Richard Nunn is the brother of Captain Chris Nunn, my son's godfather. But there is no time to mourn or even reflect, only more work coming through the door.

The second name belongs to a triumph that ends the long hard day. The CP gets a message about another Scout casevac helicopter inbound. Outside, it is blacker than Leopoldo Galtieri's heart as the boys set up six torches in the shape of a 'T'. We wait quietly in the darkness for the nasal drone of the Scout's gas turbine engine which suddenly we can hear, but in the wrong place.

The pilot has flown down San Carlos Water, stopped and turned west by dead reckoning. Slowly, agonizingly slowly, he creeps towards the beach. We switch on the lighted T for him and flash our hand torches along the front of the building, hoping that he won't take his Scout straight into the roof.

Suddenly the pilot flicks on his landing lights, then off as he sights the T, and, as if drawn to it by a piece of invisible string, the Army Air Corps pilot brings home the bacon. Even with our limited knowledge my marines and I realize we have witnessed a heroic piece of flying.

The bacon in this case is another 2 Para officer, Captain John Young. The bullet entry hole in his right flank looks ominously close to the liver, and the surrounding belly is rigid beneath Bill McGregor's questing fingers. I can see the anxiety in Bill's eyes and the personal pain. This patient is one of the officers with whom he sailed down from England in *Norland*. Now the young man is lying on a stretcher, shocked and shivering, with wide staring eyes, his blood-soaked clothing cut from his pale but well-muscled body as the Fenwal blood bags are pumped into each arm. Chief McKinley, the transfusion technician, has two more bags of chilled blood warming under his own armpits, grimacing slightly as he tries to hide his discomfort.

Four units later, Captain Young is on the table in theatre. Bill McGregor is first knife, with Charles Batty assisting. A bold slash and Bill is through a right paramedian incision and into the abdominal cavity. Dark red clot flops into the wound as the surgeon's fingers search for the bleeding point. 'There it is,' says Bill quietly, and we all crane our necks to see.

The right lobe of the liver has been gouged by a bullet. More clot is scooped out as another assistant pulls harder on the retractor that lifts the right rib cage up and away from Bill's line of sight. Some fancy needlework with deep catgut sutures, and the hole is closed, the bleeding stopped. At the head of the table Malcolm Jowitt looks well pleased with his surgeon as Bill and Charles close the belly. His smile persists as, once again, I distribute the tots for arduous duty.

Walking around the now terribly cramped facilities, a bottle in each hand to fill the proffered coffee mugs, I can see that the areas are full of post-operative patients, some now conscious following their anaesthetics, others still drowsy.

The boys on night shift, led by WO2 Brian Apperley, move quietly from stretcher to stretcher, checking, reassuring, recording and reassuring again. What a sight! I am even more conscious of the wretched bombs stuck in the ceiling and machinery next door.

There's still half a day to go on that possible time fuse, so I ask for some of the patients to be moved out of the theoretical line of flight of a detonating nose cap. The boys look at me a bit quizzically, unsure of my decision to leave apparently useful space empty down one side of the room. Then I check that the sandbags are in place. Bless their old seaboots, Bernie Bruen and his men have doubled the thickness of the sandbag wall at the critical point.

With everyone relaxed and happy, the two theatres are scrubbed out and the staff set up their bedding rolls all round the operating tables. It is definitely the right way to end the day. 47 major ops, and everyone has survived. If only I could be sure of those bombs being inert. Fifteen Paras dead though, and Richard Nunn . . .

Saturday, May 29

Another bright dawn, and the end of our first week ashore. If the air attacks continue how are we going to get our wounded out? Most of the accommodation areas have now been spilled over into by injured bodies, and we are simply running out of space. Another complication is then provided by Brigade. Reinforcement of Shelldrake, a forward position, has become a tactical priority and all available helicopters are being diverted to the task. I tell them that I don't mind, *providing* we get our Sea King back later. Our injured patients can wait a few hours more for the war effort.

A Wessex arrives and settles gently into the sodden peat. The aircrewman beckons me forward, a look of real pain and resignation on his tired face. He is sharing the helicopter's cabin with British dead – paratroopers from Goose Green. The corpses have been loaded in on top of each other, the limbs frozen in rigor mortis, and each man's combat smock or poncho cape pulled over his face.

Silently, sadly, we unload the eleven bodies, placing each corpse on its own stretcher at the side of the dressing station. There is a six-foot wide level strip of concrete running along the edge here, then a drainage ditch and high bank. The RSM of 2 Para, WO1 Malcolm Simpson, and one of the lightly injured officers who arrived this morning, a company commander, help us in the task. The two men then stand back quietly on the bank, near to tears, watching us. One by one, we strip the bodies to prepare them for burial. A pressman hovers in the background, obviously thinking about a photograph. Our thunderous looks indicate that production of a camera will result in him joining our waiting customers. I tell one of the marines to keep him and *any* other outsiders away.

The cold wet clothing is deftly cut away. The pockets are examined, and personal possessions sorted, logged and put in a plastic bag. In several cases the spare Victory berets which all the Paras seem to carry are so badly soaked with blood as to be unfit for return to the relatives. With the corpse stripped naked in the freezing air, under a clear blue sky, I then carefully examine each body to certify both death and its cause. A Field Death Certificate must be completed for each man. For one thing they had died on British soil. For another, they will all certainly require that sort of detail recorded if any of the bodies are exhumed after the war and shipped back to England. The Paras generally have strongly held views that this ought to happen, but personally I'm not so sure. Anyway, to save later examination of the bodies, particularly if a Coroner becomes involved, I must do the job properly now.

Gunshot wound of the heart, multiple gunshot wounds of chest and abdomen, blast injury. The names are burned into our memories. Dent, Bingley, Cork, Hardman, Melia, Illingsworth, Mecham, Sullivan, Holman-Smith, and finally, H himself. That same shy, quizzical smile lies on his face as easily in death as it did in life.

Like his men, the late Commanding Officer of the Second Battalion is lifted carefully into an opaque plastic liner. Gently, reverently, the shrouded corpse is then placed in the thick grey PVC body bag with its heavy zip and carrying loops. Scouse Davies writes the name on the outside, using a broad felt-tip pen, the black capital letters contrasting sharply with the shiny grey plastic of the bag.

We straighten up, our backs aching from an hour's crouching and our bloodied fingers stiff with cold. The RSM looks me in the eye, man to man, and salutes. I am confused. It has not been a pleasant task by any means, but it has been an honour for us to undertake, and we all feel satisfied that dignity has been restored to the bodies, and the memory of these brave men. At the back of my mind is the unwelcome knowledge that Richard Nunn's body has yet to be retrieved from the wreckage of his crashed Scout, and that there are another four Paras to lay out when they are recovered from Goose Green.

Back in the hospital, there is still no sign of the promised helicopter for *Uganda*. Things are getting serious because large numbers of Argentinian wounded are now arriving from the battle. Mushroom, the radio title of the duty officer at Brigade HQ, gets a headset full of polite abuse from Senior Starlight, Red Beach (me). The effect is magical.

Half an hour later Lt. Dermot Hickey arrives with a Sea King to begin three careful round trips, in between air raid warnings and actual attacks on ships in San Carlos Water. The boys see another Skyhawk creamed by a Rapier over to the west. A tremendous shout goes up as the fragments come tumbling down.

The moment that I'm dreading finally comes. Scouse informs me that the body of a dead pilot has arrived. The team forms up again. John Smith and Scouse Davies are both medical men, but John Clare, Charlie Cork, Peter Pearson and John Thurlow are general duties Royal Marines who have volunteered to help with the task of laying out bodies for burial. They are all aware of my friendship with our latest customer.

I walk round to the side again, trying to steel myself. The sheet is lifted off, and from previous experience in Northern Ireland I know what to expect, but it is still a severe shock to see the injured body of someone you have known well. Somehow I sense that I must prove to myself that Richard died *before* the crash and not *because* of it. It takes a few minutes of gentle probing, but finally I find what I am, in a way, hoping to find. There is a hole in his left cheekbone which just admits my little finger. A ricocheting bullet has penetrated my friend's face and, an instant later, his brain. This knowledge helps me to adjust – whatever happened after death, no matter how unpleasant, doesn't seem important now. I resolve at once to write to his parents, old friends who live not far from my home in Cornwall. Another neat silver bag joins the line waiting for tomorrow's funeral.

Bryn Dobbs lets me borrow his chair in the CP, a great honour. He has prepared the blank death certificates which I now complete for him. In turn he fills in the Battle Casualty Occurrence Report Forms, a painstaking task of great importance. Now that we've plugged into *Uganda* as a source of supply for medical comforts, the cigar line is once again open and flowing. As a result, my Fleet Chief's concentration is being maintained, albeit at the expense of the air which the rest of us have to breathe! The forms and certificates usually then go round to Roy Hancock in the FRO, only this time the man himself collects them. We discuss burials and the registration of graves with Roy, a subject which never really enters exercise play on Dartmoor or Salisbury Plain. It's another aspect of a war which one of my marines has described beautifully:

'Just like an exercise sir, only the umpires haven't turned up!'

There now occurs one of the hilarious moments in war that will endure long after other details have faded from memory. A piece of paper arrives which is a signal addressed to the Commando Logistic Regiment, personal for me. We have no teleprinter ashore in Ajax Bay so the thing has had to be delivered by hand. The tone is pompous, and the contents unreal:

REQUEST BETTER ASSESSMENT HELICOPTER NEEDS FOR FUTURE CASEVAC TO AVOID UNNECESSARY TASKING SCARCE ASSETS. DIFFICULTY OF ASSESSMENT UNDERSTOOD BUT MUST IMPROVE. GIVE 24 HOURS NOTICE OF FURTHER CASEVAC REQUIREMENTS.

I am speechless for a minute, then burst into laughter. The CO's reaction is exactly the same. He has seen us pack wounded survivors carefully into the Sea King and Wessex Helicopters that have turned up to help. The staff officer who has sent this signal would understand our problems exactly if he ever came to see us on the ground. Even if I lose everything else, I'll take that piece of paper back to England with me.

The Sea King returns from its third lift and shift, this time with Martyn Ward on board. He is another green-bereted MO who has come to war as Resuscitation Officer and, realistically, a battle casualty replacement if any of the Unit MOs are killed or injured. It was his turn for *Uganda* today because the surgeons are busy with Argentinian wounded from Goose Green, and he also did tremendous work round the back of the building immediately after the bombs dropped on Thursday evening.

Martyn bears gifts from *Uganda* and news. Apparently,

they are absolutely dependent on my notes for information on how things are going ashore. He has a letter for me from Surgeon Commander Mike Beeley to confirm this. They very much appreciate my sentiments that, without *Uganda*'s dedication and support, we would all be losing the battle to heal the sick and mend the injured.

I've also opened an account with *Uganda*'s Supply Officer. We've run out of whisky and rum, and I vaguely remember a paragraph in the Queen's Regulations for the Royal Navy which says that arduous duty and physical hardship can sometimes justify the purchase and issue of commercial spirit. On the strength of that vague memory we now have another half a dozen bottles.

Robert Fox, the BBC Radio Reporter turns up in the CP, looking rather tired and weary, and is immediately 'gripped' by Alan Swann. It's definitely not Robert's fault that stuff is leaking out on the World Service news bulletins. What sensible journalist would willingly reveal informed speculation about incorrect bomb fusing, when he could himself be killed by the enemy's greater attention to this problem soon after? I take Robert Fox's side in this matter, and later we have a long discussion about 2 Para's action at Goose Green, their gallant leader, and Steve Hughes' splendid work in the Regimental Aid Post. That young tiger has certainly repaid *his* fare down to the South Atlantic.

That night, Phil Shouler saves the Ajax Bay track record in a neat piece of teamwork. Despite the semi-darkness, one of the marines acting as a medical orderly draws our attention to an Argentinian patient whose face is 'looking a bit too dark boss, even for a spick'. A quick inspection with a flickering cigarette lighter shows the man to be deeply cyanosed, with complete obstruction of his larynx or voicebox, his heart just about slowed to a stop. By the light of my torch Phil then does a perfect emergency tracheostomy, butting a hole in the man's windpipe to take first an oxygen catheter, then a silver tube. The heart rate picks up immediately, pounding back to a normal rate as the oxygen floods into the deprived tissues. Another life saved, this time at the brink of extinction.

Sunday, May 30

A pleasant surprise to start the day. The personnel of No 1 Surgical Support Team from HMS *Hermes* are dumped, with all their kit, on our doorstep. It is the first time that I've seen them since early April in Plymouth. This transfer is in response to a message passed up the chain of command that we are in danger of running out of stores, particularly anaesthetics. The residents of Ajax Bay are mildly amused by the new arrivals' wearing of Red Cross armbands, and there is some light-hearted banter about this wonderful talisman which confers immunity from Skyhawks!

I know that the pressure is building up on the surgeons in *Uganda*. The techniques of battle surgery demand that high-velocity bullet and shrapnel-induced wounds should be opened up widely, cleaned out thoroughly, and *left open* while the healing process begins. We are sending explored wounds to the hospital ship, which are needing closure a week or less later. The backlog of work is becoming severe. They have asked for skilled help but have plenty of equipment. We in turn are short of kit, but could also do with an extra anaesthetist and some more theatre staff at Ajax Bay. If we could acquire those extra personnel, then the RN team could man an extra operating table, giving us a total of four.

The elegant solution is irresistible. We split up No 1 SST, sending Surgeon Commander Neville Scholes and the majority of his team straight to *Uganda*, keeping Ian Geraghty and four senior rates with us. Ian, a Surgeon Lieutenant Commander based at Haslar, is a splendid character who has already acquired an MBE for sterling work in Dominica following a disastrous hurricane. He and his men are soon happily and totally integrated into the Ajax Bay team.

Five more bodies arrive by helicopter and are laid out with the same care and devotion given to their colleagues yesterday. Life and work goes on, meanwhile, as we carry the seventeen body bags past the stockade, now filling up with nearly a thousand Argy prisoners, up the hill to where a Michigan bulldozer has carved out a broad ditch in the wet earth. This work has been carried out entirely by men of Workshop Squadron and their splendid Sergeant Major, WO2 Dave McCalley. There is no specific Graves Unit or organisation, only Royal Marines who have volunteered for this noble but unpleasant task.

The funeral itself is a fierce event. Nearly 200 men stand in silence around the edge of the mass grave, heads uncovered, the majority with hands clasped loosely in prayer. Officers mix with soldiers, Paras mingle with Royal Marines. Above us is the dome of a perfectly blue sky, while, crystal-clear in the distance, snow gleams on the summit of Mount Simon. San Carlos Water is a flat calm, the fleet lying still as the helicopters move busily from ship to ship with their loads, like bees on a summer's day. The snarl of their engines and clatter of rotor blades carry for miles in the crisp cold air. It is a beautiful spot, this carefully chosen, silent hillside.

One by one, the bodies are carried down into the grave. Eleven of the seventeen being buried today are officers or NCOs, showing exactly what the British forces mean by the word 'leadership'. Each body bag has six canvas handles, so the burial party consists of six men of similar rank to the deceased, plus one more senior escort. Major Chris Keeble, Acting CO of 2 Para, precedes the four dead officers, RSM Simpson acts for the NCOs and private soldiers. Dave Edmunds, another old friend, leads the Sapper group bearing Corporal Melia; Major Peter Cameron and several of his brother pilots carry Richard Nunn to his place of rest. Each body bag is covered by the Union Flag which is removed when the bag is in position. A silent salute, about-turn, and the burial party withdraws from the grave. When all are in place the 2nd Battalion padre, David Cooper, begins the service.

As his firm voice rolls through the now-familiar words, the emotional pressure winds up to a crescendo. Eyes that were red with tiredness and strain now brim over with silent tears that splash down on the already soggy earth.

'Ashes to ashes, dust unto dust.' The sound of handfuls of

earth cast by the RSM on to taut plastic body bags echoes like thunder around the grave. Led by Major General Moore, we all salute and slowly turn away.

I have time for a brief chat to the Royal Marines liaison officer with 2 Para. He has now taken over Battalion Intelligence, and has to return at once to Goose Green for the expected counter-attack. He is also married to Richard Nunn's sister, and grips my arm tightly when I tell him I'll be writing to the family tonight. Struggling to control his grief, he whispers a vital message: 'Tell them I was here.'

During that evening I assist Phil Shouler with his after-dusk list. As a general principle I've decided that only British casualties will be operated on during the day, unless there is a serious Argentinian case. During air raids the surgical teams should also have a chance to take cover outside the building. Another bomb into the back, *anywhere* near the two that we already have, may well cause a massive explosion. As soon as night falls, however, we know that the Mirages and Skyhawks will be unable to attack us and work can proceed unhindered.

The surgery of battle is a fascinating subject. Pieces of metal moving at high velocity when they strike flesh behave in unusual ways. A smooth and symmetrically shaped bullet sets up a shock wave which accelerates muscle and other structures away from the bullet's track. It is rather like the bow wave of a ship, and as a result, a cavity is formed for a few thousandths of a second. The pressure in this cavity is below that of the exterior, and so outside contaminants of the atmosphere are drawn in. The dying muscle tissue is therefore lined with the bugs that cause gas gangrene and tetanus, germs that simply *love* the absence of oxygen. Any surgeon foolish enough merely to tidy up the entrance and exit holes, then close them with clips or stitches, is simply asking for trouble. Infection is inevitable, and is present in all our Argentinian patients who have been treated by their own doctors in the field. Some idiot of a mendicant barber-surgeon on their side is putting clips in the wounds and giving his patients a few antibiotic tablets. But how is the penicillin supposed to penetrate dead muscle?

Our surgeons have more sense. They lay the wounds open

The *Canberra* advance party in Captain Sammy Bradford's cabin.

Canberra refuelling at sea from RFA *Tidepool*.

Fitness training: A group of Royal Marine Commandos pound the Promenade Deck of *Canberra*. The man on the right is carrying an 84mm anti-tank weapon.

Military training: *Canberra's* own Sea King Commando is unlashed prior to take-off from her midships flight deck.

First Aid training: POMA Paul Watts demonstrates the morphine syrette. Every Royal Marine and paratrooper carried one each.

SNEB rocket-equipped Gazelles training at Ascension.

HMS *Fearless* (foreground), *Canberra* and logistic ships swing at anchor off English Bay.

D-Day casualties (1). The author's Wessex helicopter lands on the foreshore of San Carlos Creek to pick up the first casualty of the land campaign — a paratrooper with an injured back.

D-Day Casualties (2). A pair of injured Argentinian soldiers, both with gunshot wounds, are tended by SBS men prior to evacuation by helicopter from Fanning Head.

The Battle of Falkland Sound. Fires blazing in her port quarter,
HMS *Ardent* lies helpless in Grantham Sound after a long day's fighting.
The author's helicopter saved two of her crew from the freezing water.

Just visible in front of HMS *Fearless'* main mast, an Argentinian Air Force Mirage (as detailed) with its port wing on fire is seconds away from crashing into San Carlos Water. The pilot did not eject.

HMS *Antelope* steams to a safe anchorage position with radio mast leaning drunkenly (struck by a low-flying A4 Skyhawk) and the hole made by a 1000lb bomb in her starboard side.

General view of the long deserted Ajax Bay mutton refrigeration plant.
Only the slaughterhouse (upper left) possessed windows.

The author paints his now-famous inscription over the main entrance to
the Ajax Bay Field Hospital.

In between air attacks. A happy trio outside Ajax Bay — WO2 Terry Moran (in helmet), POMA Eddie Middleton (seated) and FCMA Bryn Dobbs (with his usual panatella cigar).

Something nasty around the back. (Above) The author inspects a 400kg parachute-retarded UXB embedded in refrigeration machinery. (Below) A similar device lies on the compressed cork ceiling a few metres away, with a rifle laid alongside for scale.

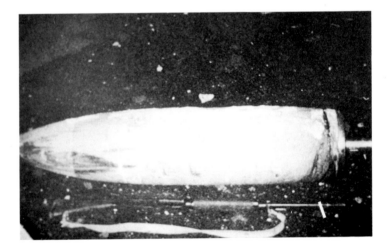

From point of wounding ... an Argentinian casualty is helped by a
fellow prisoner and Royal Marine guard.

... via light helicopter ... a Gazelle lands on the
track to pick up wounded.

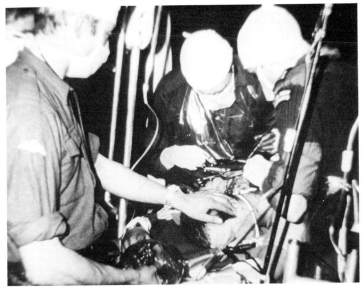

... to surgery at Ajax Bay ... Major Malcolm Jowitt of the Parachute Clearing Troop monitors the casualty's pulse while John Williams and Nick Morgan sort out his chest wound.

... and subsequent evacuation by helicopter ... Royal Marine stretcher bearers ducking under the whirling rotor blades, watched by Argentinian prisoners captured at Goose Green.

... to SS *Uganda*. The white hospital ship, known to all as 'Mother Hen', backlit by the evening sun as she steams up Falkland Sound.

The men who gave their lives for freedom. Major General Sir Jeremy Moore (with backpack, upper left) stands to attention at the edge of the grave. The author had the unpleasant but honourable task of certifying each man's death following the battle for Goose Green.

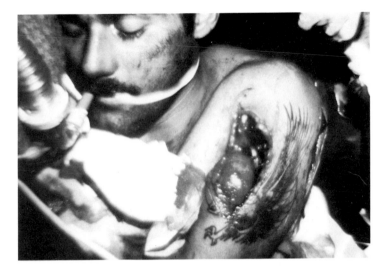

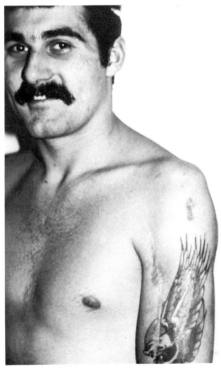

Before and after.
Corporal Jerry Phillips of
3 Para on the operating
table, June 12th. High
velocity exit wound of arm
after primary surgery —
note tattoo.

Jerry Phillips five months
later, with arm still weak
but improving daily.
(He has now recovered
completely.)

Forward Dressing Station. Stretcher bearers rush an injured guardsman from a Scout Casevac helicopter into the FDS at Fitzroy.

First view of Port Stanley. Taken from a helicopter, showing the town and inner harbour. The occupying Argentinian troops used the community centre (left foreground) as a field hospital.

London Victory Parade, with Erich Bootland (centre, dark uniform)
as part of the Royal Marines contingent.

to the air and carefully remove the dark purple pieces of dead tissue. The work is careful and thorough, demanding intense concentration and a sharp pair of scissors. Anything that is alive, even a shattered bone or crushed nerve is preserved when possible. We are simply trying to save life and limb now, so the fancy stuff with fixation bars and operating microscopes can wait until later.

When the wound is clean and glistening red, a fluffy gauze dressing gets packed in, then a crepe bandage is applied. The wounds *must* stay open for a few days more until the surgeons in *Uganda* can inspect them again. No doubt, because of the poor lighting conditions in Ajax Bay, some dead muscle will be overlooked in a proportion of the wounds. That will not matter at all, providing they remove it then. Later on they'll be able to close up the wounds neatly.

Strange that this technique was first described by Napoleon's surgeon – Joseph Larrey. He even invented the word that describes the procedure – *débridement*.

Private Manuel Caceres is Casualty No 229 and the Naval team's 34th patient. He has what looks like a mortar fragment wound of the right calf. After Ian Geraghty has put our customer to sleep, Phil Shouler invites me to explore the wound. I can feel the lump deep beneath the soleus muscle and cut down to it with my finger lying in the entry track. Surprise, surprise! A 7.62mm bullet pops out. Wonder if it's one of theirs or one of ours?

The operation takes 20 minutes, then Nick Morgan dons his gloves to debride a nasty gunshot wound of forearm and thumb. It will be his seventh operation of the day and there is one more to do before the team can scrub out the area, cover the tables with a couple of sheets, unroll their bedding, and then get their heads down until tomorrow morning.

Monday, May 31

It's the Spring Bank Holiday half a world away. Here, war goes on. The Mountain and Arctic Warfare Cadre take out an Argy Special Forces lying-up position near Top Malo House. There is a tremendous firefight, and three of the Royal Marines are injured in achieving total success. I recognize two of them, Touché Groves and Taff Doyle, both old friends from skiing and rugby days. Touché's 'magic lantern show' is a sod's opera highlight whenever he performs it, but now he's fighting for breath with a nasty chest wound. Taff Doyle comes round from his anaesthetic wanting to know if he'll still be able to 'slip his shoulder' (illegally) as a rugby hooker. Judging by his bullet-smashed upper arm I think it unlikely, but can't bring myself to say so. Another unlikely encounter takes place in the post-operative area. Two SAS men have been flown in with gunshot wounds that are obviously more than 24 hours old. We know better than to ask them about the circumstances of their injuries, instead simply operate on them. The anaesthetist uses Ketalar, a special injectable general anaesthetic with occasional interesting side effects. One of the SAS men, coming round from his op, reacts by singing bawdy rugby songs, quite tunefully, at the top of his voice! The cabaret act is much appreciated, but when I wander over to check that everything is going well, the other SAS soldier sits up and looks at me strangely. With his long hair and beard it is some seconds before I recognise him.

What a strange place for a reunion! As a teenage Royal Marine recruit, DP was in my Troop when we completed the Commando course together at Lympstone. I had heard on the grapevine that he had subsequently left the Corps, possibly to become a mercenary. Now here we were, clutching each other's hands like long-lost brothers, in the middle of nowhere. I explain this to a group of marines who are watching my strange behaviour, and they understand instantly. The sufferings endured on Woodbury Common and on the Tarzan course are severe enough to bind together men who have shared the experience for ever.

The television crews turn up. Mike Nicholson, Brian Hanrahan and Jeremy Hands all do brief interviews with me, the contents of which I cannot even recall a few minutes afterwards. The BBC cameraman, Bernard Hesketh, lingers for some time on a shot of Charles Batty in theatre, carving dead meat from the large bullet exit wound in an Argentine lieutenant's leg. It seems likely to become an image to go around the world. I sincerely hope so. The interviewers have had the truth from me, and I want the word to get back. We have a tremendous team, happy in our work but as anxious as anyone to finish the war and return home. We are *very* proud also of our track record – everyone who has made it to Ajax Bay alive has also left alive. After 107 major operations and in the face of the tremendous wounding power of modern munitions, it's no mean achievement.

As an afterthought, I mention the bombs next door. The 33 hours for the time fuses have passed and they are almost part of the furniture now. The camera crews politely decline my invitation to inspect them, but not Major General Jeremy Moore. A wiry and tough man who was once my Unit CO, it is all we can do to restrain him from taking a piece of bomb as a souvenir!

Some of our other visitors profess interest in inspection, but have usually seen enough from the door, twenty metres away. Perhaps we are all becoming slightly 'bomb-happy'. I can honestly say that we have almost forgotten about the two devices next door.

A remarkable Argentinian casualty arrives, the last from the battle of Goose Green. Private Donato Baez has just been found alive in a water-logged trench some distance from the airfield, left for dead. He has a penetrating wound of the right eye and fractures of the right hand and left thigh as well as a rigid belly and rectal temperature of 32°C. He shouldn't really be alive. Poor dumb peasant soldier – the marines feel very sorry for him and proceed to lavish tremendous care on the hapless conscript. Hot water bottles, foil blankets, fresh blood, warm Savlon for his filthy hands and feet – and the best surgeon in the South Atlantic for his wounds. His low temperature plays havoc with the anaesthetic drugs, and Malcolm Jowitt has to ventilate him by hand for two hours after Bill's operations are successfully completed. Later on in the evening, during the daily brief to all hands, I remember to mention the bombs and the possibility, now passed, of a delayed explosion. Everyone looks a bit shocked, then relieved. Good fortune still flies with us. I feel sure that the Fuerza Aerea Argentina planning staff have put a big red 'destroyed' mark through our map location, and they won't waste further airstrike efforts on us. But will we run out of ships and missiles before they run out of planes?

It all promises, as the Duke of Wellington once remarked about a different battle, to be a close-run thing.

Tuesday, June 1

For some unknown reason we can't find *Uganda* this morning. Our Sea King also fails to turn up, and discussion with Brigade HQ indicates that the heavy helicopters are now so precious that they cannot allocate one to me. Nevertheless, I can have a daily Wessex from now on! They also reassure me that *Uganda is* in her Red Cross Box, although they are not exactly sure where, and admit that the RCB represents several hundred square miles of Southern Atlantic Ocean.

Our casualty numbers in evacuation are not desperate at the moment, and the tactical forecast is quiet, so when the Wessex finally arrives I decide on a liaison run to *Uganda*. With Malcolm Jowitt in the back, along for the ride as well as looking for more anaesthetic resupply, we lift off after lunch and head out to the north, past Fanning Head. The pilot bends a few peacetime rules by allowing me, without helmet, up into the left-hand seat. He is soon enjoying the scenery as the frustrated aviator dressed as Commando doctor takes charge of the controls.

There is a rugged beauty to the Falklands coastline, and it is easy to understand why so many Royal Marines have come to love the place during their year's service here. From the cockpit of our Wessex, nose down at 100 knots as we hurtle along 60 feet above the sea, the air smells clean and the beaches look fresh and perfect as they flick past. We even see some penguins, scattering in panic as the unfamiliar and threatening clamour of a helicopter enters their lives.

'Nurse Uganda' eventually answers our radio calls after we have left the coastline way behind, and then transmits a long message for our direction-finding radio receiver. The needle on the panel indicator swings right, so I add ten degrees to our heading and settle on the new course. Another fifteen minutes, now out of sight of land, and there she is. A tiny speck on the horizon splits into three – *Uganda* is transferring patients to her attendant hospital carriers, the two converted survey ships.

I climb gradually to 500 feet as the details become clearer. We are also, hopefully, out of threat range from the enemy airstrip at Pebble Island. However, when the attack comes it is from a totally unexpected quarter. *Hecla* and *Hydra*'s Wasp helicopters break off from their tasks and head towards us. The Fleet Air Arm are at play. My pilot's instructions in the headset are brief: 'Thank you sir, I have control.'

The light of battle glints in his eyes as, watching the approaching Wasps, he times the break perfectly and cuts underneath them, rocketing back down to sea level. The small helicopters are shaken off, left well behind. Still, I am glad that the little black dots in the windscreen did not turn out to be Pucaras.

After settling on *Uganda*'s helicopter deck I unstrap and climb down. Surgeon Captain Andrew Rintoul, the Medical Officer in Charge, is there to greet us, and if he is surprised at the grubby (and in my case unshaven) creatures that salute him and shake his hand, he shows no sign of it.

In charge of the Reception/Resuscitation area at the base of the ramp is another friend of long acquaintance, Jean Kidd, normally Sister in charge of the Accident and Emergency Department of the Royal Naval Hospital back in Plymouth. She has also worked in the medical department at the Royal Marines Commando Training Centre, and is particularly fond of Ross Adley, now up front with the other medics of 42 Commando, on Mount Kent. Jean looks fresh and pretty, in marked contrast to us. She still greets us warmly, and I'll take a letter for Ross ashore with me later.

What a cool, beautiful haven this lovely ship is! From the moment that a wounded man has been stretchered down the ramp by the attendant Royal Marines Bandsmen, there is a definite feeling that *Uganda*'s staff and organization have been designed to help him heal as quickly as possible. The wards are spotless, the staff wear white plimsolls as they pad silently along the carpeted decks and, best of all, there are female nurses! The girls look divine and smell impossibly fragrant as they tend our customers of the previous week. With their faces now cleaned of camouflage cream, those patients who are not asleep grin at me as I walk past their beds, and some give a 'thumbs up' sign. I meet the various key personnel for the first time. Mike Beeley, Peter Bull, Roger Leicester and Charles Chapman are colleagues of old. Some of them turn up for tea served by the Goanese stewards. It all seems so *unreal*.

A brief conversation with MOIC and Andy Gough, the RN Commander who is also the ship's executive Senior Naval Officer, reveals a few more problems.

Tomorrow, *Uganda* is exchanging her numerous enemy patients with the *Bahia Paraiso*, her Argentinian equivalent which also shares the RCB on occasion. I explain in turn that we no longer have our high-capacity, long-range Sea Kings. However, *Canberra* is due back in San Carlos Water with the Guards and Gurkhas from *QE2*'s transfer in South Georgia. This solves the first problem as we'll be able to take today's patients to her. Andy promises to try for London's permission to get *Uganda* in much closer to us every morning afterwards. This will knock the second difficulty into touch, as we will then be able to use the Wessex for short hops of high frequency.

I take the opportunity for a quick wash, as time is limited. Hot water, from a tap! We lift off, burdened with fruit and other supplies, including a bottle of Black Label, the gift of Lt Cdr David Porteous, *Uganda*'s RN Supply Officer, who is acting as Deputy Purser. He and I shared a superb run ashore in London following an Army/Navy game at Twickenham. How marvellous it is in this small and splendid club that they call the Royal Navy to be able to reply on people whom you know and trust.

Back at base – disaster. An explosion at Goose Green in a pile of captured Argentinian ammunition has killed three prisoners and injured many more. Phil Shouler looks up, despondent, from the fresh and legless corpse he has been working on in triage. 'Sorry, boss, we lost him. Pulse was about thirty when he came in, picked up after five units of blood but it collapsed again. That's the Ajax Bay record gone.'

I am initially despondent too, then cheer him up by rephrasing our claim. Every *British* soldier who has made it to us alive has also gone out alive! Now that would be *really* something if we could still say it truthfully at the end of the war.

Some of the other casualties are ghastly. Phil asks me to help with another victim of the explosion. It seems likely that it was a booby trap set and (ironically) triggered off by Argentinians. The prisoners were quite legitimately being used to move the shells away from their position next to the schoolhouse. Our customer has lost most of one leg and suffered major damage to the other as well. Phil supervises my amputation of the left leg mid-thigh and the preparation of a reasonable stump. The right leg takes much more time as we tease out lumps of molten plastic and dirt, blades of grass, and small pieces of jagged shrapnel from the charred and bleeding muscle. It is a real horror show and I can appreciate even more the sustained quality of the surgical team's efforts.

During our flight back from *Uganda*, Malcolm Jowitt had discussed with me the possibility of getting some of the fitter Argentinian prisoners to donate their blood. His idea now becomes critical because apparently we are running very short of fresh red cells. There is a problem however. The senior Army officer in their compound has refused point-blank to allow any of his men to co-operate. I ask for Colonel Pioggi to be brought in immediately. Malcolm acts as escort.

With typical Argy bravado, the colonel swaggers into theatre, behaving as if he is the landlord rather than a guest. At the critical moment I step to one side and give him the full, Technicolor visual impact of Patient 275's dreadful wounds. The message to him via our interpreter is clear, and translates perfectly into Spanish: 'Sir. Some *bastard* boobytrapped the ammunition dump in Goose Green. This is one of your men, and there are others. We need more fresh blood.'

The bald-headed senior officer sways on his feet, unable to look any longer at the gore and blackened meat. He turns away, muttering in Spanish: '*Cuánto – cuál tipo?*' Malcolm and his team then set to again. The corridor that acts as their transfusion clinic is narrow, dusty and poorly lit, but two hours later Chief McKinley returns with better news. There are 60 pints in the bag now with as much again available 'on the hoof' if necessary, and the blood crisis is over. Colonel Pioggi has been so badly shaken by his visit to theatre and our obvious efforts for his men that he has lost all his previous surliness and haughty attitude. He has also told his own explosives expert to have a little talk with Flt Lt Swann. Some surprising facts emerge later from this technical tête-à-tête, and it is another good way to end a bad day in the meat market.

Wednesday, June 2

Missed breakfast after oversleeping. There's a low mist, with thick fog lying on San Carlos Water. The helicopters are unable to fly this morning, at least until the sun gets high enough to burn off some of the clag. The absence of chattering rotor blades and whining engines has allowed extended time in the arms of Morpheus. Still, I have the persistent feeling throughout the day that I was actually dreaming about being asleep, before waking up to find that it wasn't true.

The Amphibious Beach Unit confirm the rumours. *Canberra* is in, a mile in front of *Fearless* and out of sight to us in the sheltered recess of Ajax Bay. One of the theatre Petty Officers, Fleet Chief Bryn Dobbs and I hijack a cheerful Royal Marines coxswain and his rigid raider for the brief ride out to the liner. She looks even more weatherbeaten than last week, following her journey to South Georgia. There will certainly be no cruising brochure photography today. A short chat with Surgeon Captain Roger Wilkes confirms some details, and precedes a much longer brief to all the *Canberra* medical staff, in his cabin, about events since we parted company on D-Day. There is much to tell on both sides.

FRW insists that I should use his bath facilities as I am undoubtedly no pleasure to be downwind of. The bath water looks like black railway-canteen coffee by the time I've finished, but the feeling of cleanliness is uplifting. Culinary standards are as high as ever in the Pacific Restaurant and the staff just as cheerful. In the Bonito Room they have now taken our Argentine Special Forces wounded, as well as the victims of the Goose Green booby trap incident.

Everything looks busy and efficient as I return ashore with FRW to show him around Ajax Bay. His reaction to the guided tour of the set-up is quite different to that of another senior officer who, having been cocooned in *QE2* and remote

106

from the first ten days of our little war, walks into Reception, looks around, laughs and says:

'Well, *this* isn't how we planned it!'

Now the 45 Commando and 3 Para have passed through Teal Inlet on their long 'yomp' across the northern part of the island, it will soon be time to move medical assets forward, along with other logistic bits and pieces. Malcolm Hazell will be taking an advance party around there tonight on an LSL. They'll be reinforced later by Charles Batty's Field Surgical Team. We won't get any extra operating capability to replace them for the moment, but at least Erich Bootland's Troop can now come ashore from *Canberra*. It's like a complicated game of musical hospital beds, with limited facilities being spread as thinly as possible to keep some kind of service going in two locations.

Another Argentine soldier nearly croaks on us. A Cabo (Corporal) slips into deep coma following an operation to remove shell splinters from his leg. Nothing seems capable of waking him, and his snoring respirations get more and more shallow and less and less frequent. Although his eye reflexes appear normal, we begin to wonder about the possibility of some kind of exotic brain damage. For the patient's sake, as well as trying for one of Father Mulcahy's 4077th MASH-type miracles, we call for a cleric. Without a Roman Catholic padre of our own, we have to rely on the Argentinian priest captured at Goose Green. Inspecting our patient, he sees the need immediately and performs the Last Rites. By now our man is pretty far gone, his mouth forming an enlarged 'O', death apparently only a matter of hours away. I certainly don't expect him to be around in the morning.

Thursday, June 3

Not only is the NCO alive, he's well! It's an incredible transformation from last night. The man is sleeping quietly on his side, and is easily rousable. *Muchas gracias*, Don Mulcahy! It's not only in television scripts that miracles come true. Like the others, our Argentinian Lazarus goes to *Uganda*, along with some fresh blood landed from *Canberra*'s replenished stocks.

The P&O medical and nursing staff from *Canberra* also come ashore to look around, take photographs and be amazed by the guided tour. Peter Mayner very kindly leaves a crate of beer for the lads. It's one can per three men later, and never were a few mouthfuls of cold Australian lager more gratefully accepted.

In the afternoon I feel like doing some painting to celebrate Ajax Bay's success, so climb up above the entrance doorway with a pot of red gloss. For some obscure reason, Marine Fraz Coates has a small paint-brush in his ambulance tool kit. The bold, foot-high letters are blocked in for all to see:

WELCOME TO
THE RED AND GREEN
LIFE MACHINE

That night our first of a new type of casualty comes in, a young marine of 42 Commando who stepped on the edge of a buried anti-personnel mine during offensive patrolling in the area of Mount Kent. The front half of his boot is completely shredded and the mangled remains of his fore-foot has flapped back on itself. The nineteen-year-old man has a positive mental attitude:

'Lucky really, sir, didn't get it quite right. If I'd stood on the bugger properly I'd have lost it all at the knee.'

Well done, Royal. Without any help, he's taken the first big step back on the road to normality.

There is more encouragement too with a message from *Uganda* written by four of the casualties from our bombing. Their letter is taped to the reception area wall for the boys to see and feel proud as much of the men who sent it as of their own efforts

Mne Watt
Mne Burnett
Mne Cragg
Mne Mudge

To: Surgn Cdr Jolly and all the officers and men of the
     medical team ashore at Ajax Bay

Dear Sir,

On behalf of the lads injured in the attack on Ajax Bay on the evening of 27th May and now on board the SS UGANDA, I'd like to thank you and your fantastic team for saving our lives and limbs. You cannot ever know how much we appreciate it, you were all great. Please pass on our gratitude to *all* the staff for doing such a marvellous job. Thanks a million. Take care.

Yours sincerely,
Gerry Watt
(Royal Marines Ordnance Squadron)

Friday, June 4

Dreadful day, with heavy rain. Spend much of the afternoon with Surgeon Captain Blackstone, bringing him up to date on events so far. For some reason it appears to be raining *inside* the triage area as well. Beads of rainwater form on the ceiling and fall in muddy puddles on the floor. We must get up into the roofspace somehow, and stop the leak. Corporal John Clare and I find a trapdoor in the dimly lit main corridor and lever ourselves up. There is a loud drumming sound as the sheets of rain strike the galvanized tin roof. Because of the wind's direction, some of the rainwater is coming straight in through a hole in the upper part of the front wall, the one made on May 27 when we were visited by the Argy Air Force. The cork insulating material lying above the ceiling and beneath the hole has absorbed some of this, but the soggy pool is now overflowing.

At the base of the hole I also find a piece of twisted, shining metal. Peering through the hole, and aligning my gaze with an oval split in the roof behind me, I'm staring at the shallow crater outside that also appeared on May 27, just after I had dived into the nearby sangar.

We plug the hole with cork blocks, stop the leak, and descend to ground level again. Flight Lieutenant Alan Swann confirms my worst fears. The piece of twisted metal is part of the tail fin of one those Matra parachute-retarded devices! Bomb number four therefore struck the tin roof; crossed the space above the main reception and operating area on a descending track, parallel to and about three feet away from a main joist; impacted with the front wall, nose cap on, passing through without detonating; bounced on the ground, travelling at a couple of hundred miles an hour, again without detonating, and finally – ended up on the beach.

If it had gone off as advertised in the maker's brochure, it would have killed us all, patients, staff, the lot. Who would have tended the injured? The war would have gone on, of course, but what a price to pay in morale as well as medical assets. The incident doesn't bear thinking about in depth – just praise the Almighty for small mercies and get on with the job. Humour, of course, plays an important part once again. I show the piece of crumpled bomb fin to Bernie Bruen and the Naval divers, now successful conquerors of UXBs in *Sir Galahad* and *Sir Lancelot*. They suggest that I mount the thing on a wooden plinth, and lend it to the Tate Gallery as a piece of abstract sculpture entitled 'Adrenalin is Brown'!

Saturday, June 5

I've been affected by the PCT virus. Their disease has finally cracked me! This morning I climb out of my sleeping bag and, without thinking, start to clean my shoes. The Para medics laugh heartily at my adoption of the first of their basic and reflex routines, but I draw the line at wasting water by shaving.

Another quiet day with not much happening. We tidy out the whole building as best we can, but the choking clouds of dust which rise in response to our new *Canberra*-donated brooms make cleaning the floor area very difficult.

The Fuerza Aerea Argentina Medical Officer who has been helping us look after prisoners, reveals an interesting side of his character as well as the way in which Argentine officers regard their soldiers. We have allowed Lt Miranda free access from his compound to the medical areas, providing he has an escort to take him there and back. Tonight I wonder if he's had supper, and ask him to accompany me outside and share a mess tin. I join the galley queue, as usual, and I'm suddenly aware of his surprise and change of attitude. In halting English he explains he cannot understand why the 'Commandante' of the hospital should have to stand in line for food. With our language difficulty I try to explain to him that no British officer would ever eat until he was sure that his men had eaten too, but this is a concept of operations quite beyond his understanding.

Sunday, June 6

Church parade, Father John Ryan of HMS *Intrepid* comes ashore and holds an inter-denominational service in the main treatment area which is well attended. Bernie Bruen's fiddle doubles as church organ for the occasion, and proper musical accompaniment makes a great difference to the standard of hymn singing.

We start the day with an 'Air Raid Red' warning long before dawn, followed by the sound of an Argentinian Canberra jet dropping bombs somewhere in the distance, but then the clag and rain set in again and we're spared further attention. Later, the rain clouds clear, to be replaced by high winds which make flying very difficult for the casevac Wessex helicopter, and severely tests our pilot. He rises to the occasion, and *Uganda* gets her customers without additional injuries.

A Gazelle is shot down over to the east by some kind of Argentinian missile. The four occupants are killed instantly but the paperwork has to be completed. It's a macabre task, but the team do their jobs quietly and reverently. The forms and certificates are filled in, collated and sorted, and the details beamed back to London on the satellite. Curtains will be twitching on the married patch at Middle Wallop. Three widows' doors for someone to knock on, and a mother to be informed that her son is now a permanent part of military history. Still, it could happen to any one of us. Let's roll the Argies up and get on home, before there are too many more to examine and bury.

Monday, June 7

Not a cloud in sight as the sun comes up in the clear, cold sky of San Carlos. I see from the diary that I have a speaking engagement this morning in the Training Division at the Royal Naval Hospital, Plymouth! Too late to send apologies – but then most of my potential audience are probably down here anyway.

One occasional feature of cloudless days is that we can see, from the ground, the long white vapour trails of a high-flying aircraft. These are just like the contrails over south-west England left in the track of big passenger jets heading out over the Atlantic to the New World. This morning something is wrong, because HMS *Exeter* springs into life. With a bang that is clearly audible inside the buildings at Ajax Bay, she launches a Sea Dart missile at a fast-moving contrail passing from south to north above Falkland Sound.

I race outside to watch, and am met by a group of chortling, sarcastic Royal Marines. The missile began to climb, then went 'rogue' and either fell with toppled gyros into the Sussex mountains behind us, or else was steered there under limited control.

'Useful bit of matelot kit, eh boss. Sea Dart? I'll give you Sea Dart. More like Sea Fart I reckon!'

More roars of laughter as the boys try to stop their steaming mugs of tea from spilling on the ground. As the rocket's smoke drifts away we can still see the steady white line moving across the sky above us. In San Carlos Water the scene looks peaceful, the destroyer lying quietly out in the middle of a glassy anchorage. I am about to say something about Type 42s having a *twin* Sea Dart mounting when, with a whoosh and bang that echo around the hills, a second missile leaps upwards from its launch rail. With a silent, awesome grace it climbs fiercely, sprinting towards a target which is now obliterated from us by the exhaust plume. We stand in silence beneath the steadily decreasing roar, until suddenly someone says: 'Jesus Christ – the poor bastards.'

As the white cloud of the missile's trail drifts away with the wind, we can now see that the thin line of its target's contrail has stopped abruptly. The tumbling fragments of wing and fuselage are invisible to us as they fall against the velvet-blue backdrop. Canberra bomber? Photo-recce Learjet? Who knows – but the crew must have seen their deaths coming for ten or fifteen seconds. What a way to die! Hope they had ejector seats, but well done *Exeter*, anyway. Once again we are up against the paradox of war. We can admire our enemies, even respect their courage and skill, but also cheer when they are removed violently from the battlefield.

The daily Wessex arrives but we have no custom for *Uganda* today. With everything quiet in the shop, and Tim Hughes, today's pilot, keen to keep his hand in, we indulge in a spot of contour flying down to Goose Green. The intercom is unserviceable so, in the back, I relax initially as we tear along close to the bleak terrain. The sheep and wild horses scatter in all directions as we flash past. What war? Mount Usborne has a close covering of snow and looks deceptively close in the middle distance. But now we are away from the mutual protection systems of San Carlos. Dragging my eyes back to acquisition range, I try to be serious about the threat of Pucara. The Argy home-brew turbo-prop aircraft hunt in pairs and are well-armed, and we know that there are still some left in Port Stanley. Nice target, a fat little Wessex on its own. I finger the cocking handle of our port-mounted GPMG uneasily, and try not to think about Richard Nunn's last, desperate fight.

The main purpose of today's trip is to check that all is well medically with Goose Green's garrison, now transferred from 2 Para to 1/7 Gurkhas. That doesn't take long, so then we land on the airfield and take some snaps of the two derelict Pucaras that sit there. Farther on we photograph the grave of Lieutenant Nick Taylor, the Sea Harrier pilot who was shot down while attacking the airstrip in May. The cross is wooden and beautifully made, the grave tucked in behind a fence at the far edge of the field. I find a manageable piece of an Argentine Navy jet as well, part of a pile of wreckage strewn around in the undershoot. The downwash of our main rotor blades flicks this piece of fuselage over to show the letters 'ARMAD' of Armada (Navy) on its camouflaged outer surface. The souvenir is quickly acquired and brought back to Ajax Bay.*

In the interim we've had a young man in with a bad bullet wound of the chest. Unfortunately, this was an 'accidental discharge'. He is rather unwell as Nick Morgan, John Williams and Malcolm Jowitt get to work. Later, their patient will probably complain about the three tubes inserted into his chest. but now these drainage routes do a vital job in carrying away the blood leaking from the long bullet track. Lucky boy – he's another survivor, and against the odds.

The mail arrives. Nothing for me, so temporary gloom while the duty staff in the CP tear into news from home. We have some stores to go forward to Teal Inlet, the harbour on the northern flank that is acting as logistics base for the assaults on Mounts Kent and Longdon as well as Two Sisters. Chief Petty Officer Jethro Young, and one of the PCT corporals, accompany the boxes of dressings, drugs, a sack of mail, and a morale-boosting pair of whisky bottles.

The push forward of men and equipment from San Carlos continues. Each night either *Fearless* or *Intrepid* disappears around to Fitzroy with her tank decks full of men and supplies. The off-loading can be very tricky if the weather turns unpleasant, but there doesn't seem to be any real alternative. The overland route from Fitzroy to Bluff Cove, the next settlement up the line, is along nine miles of difficult track. To the North, HQ LFFI have kept a couple of LSLs moving around into Teal Inlet, and one is busy unloading as we arrive over the bunkhouse after a twenty-minute flight. Tim settles the Wessex down above the Day-Glo landing panels secured to the wet ground in the corner of the adjoining field.

Inside the Forward Dressing Station, as the bunkhouse is now called, Malcolm Hazell and his men seem both cheerful and comfortable. With running hot water they have every reason to be, but conditions are still very cramped and

* This is now in the Fleet Air Arm Museum at Yeovilton.

they've been forced to rig two large tents outside, blistered on to the main building, to provide extra space. Charles Batty and Dick Knight have also brought their Forward Surgical element of the PCT up to Teal Inlet and, supported by the resuscitative skills of Tim Riley, Howard Oakley and the others, they look ready to tackle anything. Most important of all, the Senior Rates are in good heart, especially CPOMA 'Nutty' Edwards. It is usually pretty easy to pull his leg or, as Royal Marines would say, 'get a bite' out of him, and the unfortunate Chief doesn't let us down. Jethro Young says it's not even sport any more. There are no worries about this bunch.

As we board the Wessex again for our flight back, I notice a small, sad procession moving out from the hamlet. At its head is the padre, striding out. Just behind him is the flag-draped body bag containing the mortal remains of Sergeant Kiwi Hunt. The Special Boat Squadron are burying their dead in the weak sunlight of a Falklands winter afternoon. Cradling their Ingram sub-machine pistols, long-haired, wild-eyed and wearing a variety of outdoor and Alpine clothing, their general appearance is bizarre to those onlookers totally ignorant of their methods and skills. Today they stop the war for an hour to pay their respects to a dead Royal Marines comrade. From over 400 metres I salute without embarrassment, and climb back up into the cabin.

Flogging back at low level to San Carlos there is time to notice how different the terrain is here. Layers and layers of long white tussock grass flick in the wind and the pale yellow light. Tim diverts the aircraft slightly towards the coast, and then tightens into a 360-degree turn so that we can see a colony of penguins on a clean spit of sand below. We stay high enough not to frighten them too much, then coast back down to San Carlos Water.

Another funeral, this time of the four Gazelle crewmen killed yesterday. Once again, Workshops Squadron do their honourable thing and dig a beautiful grave for the officer, sergeant and two men to lie in together, united in death in the blinding flash of an anti-aircraft missile explosion.

Later that evening the CO describes Division's plan. The final assault will begin on the nights of June 10/11 and 11/12.

117

By then 5 Brigade will be in position on the southern flank, ready to assault Tumbledown, Harriet and Mount William, and draw a steel noose even tighter around the defences of Port Stanley. Tonight the remainder of the Welsh Guards are journeying around in one of the LSLs, having being unable to make a rendezvous with the landing craft last night when they made the trip in *Fearless*.

The sooner they get there and make their way to the start line, the better. The boys in the north, on the slopes of Longdon, Kent and Two Sisters, are starting to suffer from the effects of exposure from the cold and wet. We are now seeing marines and paras with trench foot, an insidious World War I vintage problem that we are reasonably familiar with. The proper description for the condition is 'non-freezing cold injury', but that is a heartless accountant's way of describing the myriad changes brought on by night after night in the open at sub-zero temperatures, with boots that never dry out properly and socks that are never warm even when stuffed in armpits and groins. Men who got their feet seawater wet to start with, like 2 Para, are suffering even more. The salt crystals in their boot leather act like magnets to further moisture. Why can't we get right an unglamorous but critical item like boots, in this modern era of microprocessor technology and satellite communications?

A small number of men are broken by the pain in their feet and are casevaced to Ajax Bay. We attempt to give them the dryness and warmth that their damaged limbs need. It's not always successful, and every morning John Williams has the heartbreaking task of selecting those in Evac who must now go to *Uganda* after failing to improve. Some of the young marines and paras are almost in tears, because they know the *Uganda* is Red Cross territory and that they will be out of the final battle as a result, unable to return.

Later, someone is to suggest to me that trench foot is the 'latest way to get out of the war', possibly because of the speed with which signs improve under the ideal conditions on board *Uganda*. My reaction to this slur on the integrity of the Paras and Commandos, as well as John Williams' clinical judgement, is rather vehement.

His later apology is more graceful when he understands

the background to the story. If only we had *Canberra* back in as a rest and recreation facility in San Carlos, we could prolong this war indefinitely. The men with serious symptoms would be treatable, and those who were about to become serious could be forestalled. Judging from the condition of some of the troops evacuated from the front line with trench foot, and hearing their stories, there are many others in the hills with the same problem. Up front, men are suffering silently in the certain knowledge that other members of the section or platoon are similarly afflicted. In their mutual discomfort, they are all equally reticent about declaring it.

If it was true last week to wonder whether we would run out of ships before the Argies ran out of aircraft, then this week's theme must be the possibility that we will run out of capable feet before the order is given to cross the start line. I make my feelings known to Ivar Hellberg, who comes to inspect Evac and goes away looking very thoughtful. The sooner we get going on Stanley the better.

Tuesday, June 8

30 minutes after first light the daily Wessex launches from Ajax Bay with a load of injured. HQ LFFI, or Division HQ as it is sometimes called, had promised that *Uganda* would be close in this morning because of her absence yesterday. Foolishly, I believe them without checking first. With its fuel almost exhausted from inspecting Grantham and Falkland Sounds, the Wessex returns and lands outside the door once again. The wounded try to hide their disappointment and pain. Div. HQ reply to my ill-concealed fury with a 'Wait – Out'. An hour later there is a different voice on the net as the Watch-keeping Officers change over. Perhaps they have been too busy to discuss my 'minor' problem of *Uganda*'s whereabouts? Once again, the word from on high is 'Wait – OUT.'

The time has come to investigate *Intrepid*'s potential as a large-scale hospital by using the flight deck, ramp and tank deck instead of the wardroom up forward. Bill McGregor, Erich Bootland, Ian Geraghty and I take a ride to the LPD where we are met by a very frosty Royal Marines major, the Amphibious Operations Officer. He must think this is all a fantastic plot to undermine him, because apparently this is the first time that he has even heard of the floating hospital plan! I am very surprised by this news and say so to Captain Dingemans, the model of courtesy and hospitality up in his cabin.

From our brief inspection of *Intrepid*, our feelings concur with the Captain's. His ship could certainly be made into an emergency medico-surgical facility and parked in Barclay Sound, to the north of Port Stanley, but it would be a poor choice. No seafarer likes to be static and anchored while at war. Equally worrying are the large quantities of engineer stores tucked away down below. These will obviously be needed for the rebuilding of Stanley. So why ditch them, to make room for emergency hospital facilities that may not themselves be required for anything other than the short term?

After a quick lunch we all pop over to *Atlantic Causeway* by landing craft. The sister of the ill-fated *Atlantic Conveyor* is a far better bet. The ship has three, large empty vehicle decks, a lift and helicopter platform. How close can she get into Port Stanley? The rest of the party fly back to Ajax Bay, thanks to a friendly passing Wessex crew, while I journey to *Fearless* by rigid raider, to find some answers to my questions.

The responsible Staff Officer on board is apologetic. The '*Intrepid*/floating hospital' concept has just gone out of fashion, although not dismissed entirely. He asks me instead to look at Goose Green as a more suitable location for the field hospital, because here we'll be just a little closer to the front lines around Stanley. There is no serious objection to this plan apart from the overcrowding already extant at Goose Green. Bombs, or no bombs, Ajax Bay still looks like good value.

Further discussion is interrupted by an 'Air Raid Red' warning. I finish my coffee at carpet level and am then distressed to hear Captain Jeremy Larken's tannoy information about HMS *Plymouth* being hit. For the next ten or fifteen minutes he keeps his ships' company silent at their duties with a description of the battered Rothesay Class frigate limping into the anchorage under a cloud of smoke, listing to starboard but apparently refusing help. Then the tone changes. They are short of fire fighters and breathing apparatus, so Captain Larken begins to muster his resources and prepare to get them across.

Back aft in Flyco, I chat to Lt Cdr Ed Featherstone, *Fearless*'s Aviation Oficer. My suggestion that the request for fire fighters will probably mean casualties, in need of evacuation, is seized on gratefully by the Command on the bridge. Within minutes I'm on my way to the stricken frigate in a commandeered Wessex.

Shades of *Ardent*! It's like May 21 and D-Day all over again, only this time there are no fires apparent, only smoke pouring from the mortar well, flight-deck hangar and funnel. Fire-fighting hoses snake across the flight deck as HMS *Avenger* pulls along the starboard side to play cooling streams on to the hottest danger areas. Our only access point is up on the foredeck, in front of the gun turret, so I'm winched down here.

On the slippery deck surface the main rotor downwash threatens to push me over the side but I have time, as I struggle to regain balance, to notice a pile of empty shell cases beneath the twin 4.5 inch mountings. HMS *Plymouth* has been in a stiff fight.

The bridge staff look pale and dazed beneath their anti-flash hoods as they wrestle with damage control problems. It takes me a minute to manoeuvre the Neil Robinson stretcher through the starboard wing, and aft into the main passageway below. There is just time for a cheerful salute in transit to Captain David Pentreath, then the acrid smoke engulfs our faces. I'm soon choking, with fiercely watering eyes, and only manage to continue by tying a towel scarf around my face.

In the main passageway, or 'Burma Road', the fire fighters are briefing carefully in their fearnought suits and wearing compressed-air breathing apparatus. There is a clear layer of air next to the deck along which a man can crawl in comfort. The fire fighters are cool and collected – the whole thing could almost be just another Portland damage control exercise. Probably the best way to play it.

In the wardroom the ship's medical staff are busy. *Avenger*'s MO is here too, as they tend to one man with severe smoke inhalation, another with a fractured arm, and a third with a broken lower leg. Lying against a bulkhead is the most severely injured member of the ship's company, a stoker with a depressed fracture to his skull. Sticking out of the top of his head is a piece of metal support bracket, embedded in the bone. The man needs Bill McGregor, and soon.

Carefully I lead him up on to the main deck level, having passed the stretcher up another companionway. One of the First Aid Party helps me strap in our patient, and we carry him aft to the sloping flight deck. The list to starboard appears much greater now – perhaps they are counter-flooding. No problem for the Sea King which comes right in over the deck, until we can practically hand up the stretcher to the waiting crewman. Five minutes later we're round the corner, and once again walking into the Red and Green Life Machine.

So concerned am I about HMS *Plymouth* and my chance involvement with her problems, it takes me a little while to realize that nobody wants to know about happenings in San Carlos. Some terrible event has occurred down on the southern flank with rumours of 40 or 50 men from 45 Commando dead!

Gradually the picture emerges. The LSL *Sir Galahad* has been bombed by Skyhawks while anchored near Fitzroy, *Sir Tristram* is involved too. There are large numbers of casualties, including some of our sister organisation, 16 Field Ambulance. A Gazelle gunner rushes in with a scribbled note from the CO of 16 Fd Amb:

RICK
GALAHAD HIT BEFORE SURGICAL TEAMS UNLOADED.
MANY (NOT YET COUNTED) BURNS CASUALTIES. NEED FLUIDS
AND MORPHIA PLUS PLUS.
                    JOHN ROBERTS.

We respond to this *cri-de-coeur* as best we can. John Williams grabs some kit and flies off immediately in the waiting Gazelle. Mike von Bertele follows soon after in a Scout, with several fluids resupply boxes.

Slowly, things degenerate into a nightmare. As night creeps over the horizon, load after load of helicopter casualties begin to arrive at Ajax Bay. Each patient seems worse than the last, until soon the triage and resuscitation areas are completely choked. Helicopters continue to clatter in, and stretcher-borne casualties keep appearing in the main door. No one knows how many are coming, only that we've had over 120 victims of the bombing, mostly with burns.

The phrase 'Mass Casualty Situation' flicks into the forefront of my memory. By NATO definitions, this is said to have occurred when an overwhelming number of incapacitated or injured people arrive in a limited medical facility which cannot cope with them. Hell, we can cope with *some* of them, and we are duty-bound to try and bring the greatest benefit to the biggest number. I race down to Log HQ and get on the radio to Division. We ask them, urgently, to prepare a list of ships that can take up to a *hundred* lightly injured. The number staggers the Duty Officer, but by the time he queries it I'm back in the hospital. Paddy George takes over negotiations.

Mercifully, at around 150, the numbers begin to slow. With ten from *Plymouth* that means 160 injured, standing or lying around in the building. The teams get to work on the more severely afflicted as Paddy's runner comes up with a message. *Fearless, Intrepid* and *Atlantic Causeway* are standing by to receive two dozen injured each. Bless them. Colour Sergeant McDowell then produces the necessary landing craft from somewhere, and we're in business. It's the old human nature bit of helping out your mates – people turn up from the most unexpected quarters and offer their services.

The Welsh Guardsmen are stoical and cheery as we break the news to them. Standing near the doorway, blowing on their tattered and painful hands to keep them cool, many are pathetic sights. The skin hangs from the fingers like thin white rags, their faces are blistered and raw, their hair singed short. But by God, they're brave. The bad news of another half hour in an LCU, before they can be treated, is simply and willingly accepted. Each man seems to know of someone else in the building more seriously injured than himself, and all would rather see him treated first. It's heartbreaking to turn nearly 70 young men away from the casualty department door that they have paid so much to reach, but there is no other way.

With the serious overcrowding problem solved now, it is an all-out effort for the burned and wounded. A simple treatment plan evolves, ordered by a medical officer, and carried out by either a medical assistant, or more frequently, one of the marines. Bernie's divers turn up as well, to lend their capable and willing hands. For each patient there is one attendant, sometimes two. It's a heartening sight. The fused and charred clothing is cut away, and the total percentage of burned skin area assessed and recorded. Where necessary an intravenous infusion is set up. Then carefully and lovingly, Flamazine is spread thickly over the affected areas. The cool white cream contains a silver and sulpha drug mixture which is pain-killing, antiseptic and promotes healing. Hands and fingers are enclosed in sterile plastic bags to avoid the risks of

124

bandaging. If a scar forms under a dressing it will probably remain undetected until too late, and a contracture might be the severe and unwelcome penalty.

In the worst cases, Phil Shouler and the other surgeons perform escharotomies, deliberately slitting the sides of each bloated finger to prevent strangulation of the digital circulation.

The floor of Ajax Bay seems ankle deep in rubbish, littered with torn packets and cellophane wrappings. We run out of Flamazine on the last patient, a Guardsman with flash-burnt forearms. Bryn Dobbs then remembers that he has a tube of the stuff secreted in his first aid kit, so retrieves it. There is now less than an ounce for any further casualties, so let's hope that's it for the night.

Division are being obtuse again, unable to grasp the sheer magnitude of our problem and even querying our need for *Uganda* tomorrow morning! A one-syllable word picture to the poor duty Mushroom brings him up to date at the rush, and all is understood. Someone told him that *Uganda* had been in Middle Bay throughout today, without any business! An hour later he is back on net with welcome news from London. *Uganda* will be close in, at first light. I thank him gratefully and forget our differences.

One of the chaps in charge of prisoners starts to behave like an idiot and also needs 'picturising', in the vernacular of the Corps. Apparently ignorant of events on our side of the building, he demands to know why our galley is not serving hot meals at the usual time! He is shown the galley staff spreading Flamazine on burned faces rather than margarine on dry biscuits, but continues to grumble. As a result, he's invited from now on to use the main galley, 200 muddy metres away, instead of ours.

The boys have all earned their tots tonight. John Williams is very worried about the lad from *Plymouth* with smoke inhalation damage to his lungs. Steroids and bottled oxygen seem to be holding the problem at bay, but even in the dim light of a string of 60 Watt light bulbs it's easy to see the cyanotic bluish tinge of the young sailor's lips. Captain Terry McCabe and WO2 Brian Apperley, Big Brian, lead the nursing effort. Once again there is a constant round of soothing, checking,

125

adjusting, recording and checking again. The marines have been simply magnificent throughout. One little group containing Jan Mills and Jock Inglis are secretly very pleased to have survived the test and done so well. Their delight is typically expressed in a slightly oblique fashion, tinged as usual with Corps humour:

'Boss, now that we've passed the practical, how's about getting some theory?'

Wednesday, June 9

An hour before dawn I get up and walk around. Most patients appear to have had a comfortable night, although some of the Chinese crew are beginning to suffer badly. Their faces seem to have swollen more with flash burning than the Europeans – perhaps they were closer to the bombs or received the detonation in a different way. Two of the worst have blackened Buddha-like visages. Our priority list is going to be very difficult once the daily Wessex appears.

Remembering yesterday's first mistake I brief the pilot out on the LS before he has time to shut down, and he duly lifts up over the Sussex Mountains to search for *Uganda*. Within minutes he's back, thumbs up! The crewman shows me the hospital ship's location on the map. She's in Grantham Sound, near the southern end of Falkland Sound, the scene of *Ardent*'s gallant last hours.

John Williams escorts the first flight and takes a short letter for Surgeon Captain Rintoul. I warn *Uganda*'s MOIC to expect 150 casualties throughout today, then confirm the arrangements with Division. We'll empty Ajax Bay first, then the three ships that were so helpful in our hour of need last night. The Wessex leaves, and a dark blue Sea King arrives. I rub my eyes in amazement, since I recognize the dulled-over fuselage number of a training aircraft from the Naval Air Station at Culdrose in Cornwall. I had no idea that these helicopters had been mobilized and deployed down South. The aircrewman recognizes me too, so while they're waiting to begin another task they willingly take on a load for *Uganda*. And so the pattern goes on throughout the day. Working their little secret communications nets between them, crew after crew lands outside Ajax Bay with the pilot having 'heard a buzz' and asking 'Anything we can do to help?'

With only one Wessex formally tasked to us, and with that

kind of cheerful assistance from the other Fleet Air Arm support helicopters, we shift the 160 patients to *Uganda* by mid-afternoon. It is a tremendous effort by everyone concerned, not the least *Uganda* herself. According to John Williams they're all shaken and silent, but determined. Thank God they are there.

One of the returning helicopters brings the Red Cross inspection team ashore. They are concerned with prisoners' welfare and conditions, and although well-versed on points of International Law, the team of three men and one woman seem to have a strange grip on the realities of life in the Falklands. Their leader enquires politely where he can hire a car to drive to Port Stanley, and seems very surprised when shown the trackway outside as being the only road for many miles! Our dusty accommodation is not to their liking either, and as there are no hotels locally which take American Express, they fly back to *Uganda* in their three-piece suits and tailored wellies.

But not before the prisoners have had a go at them. A couple of Huey pilots complain that they have to sleep in the same building as an unexploded bomb! Another pilot, the Pucara flight commander at Goose Green, thinks he should still have his flying helmet. Ungrateful chap, that Major Tromba. I've given him the address of Martin-Baker Ltd in England in a direct swap for his bonedome.* As he's used one of Martin-Baker's ejection seats for real, pursued by a trio of hungry Sea Harriers, the Argentinian pilot has only to write and claim his special tie and tankard.

Some Field Ambulance officers and men turn up to be accommodated with us. Major Jim Ryan, a quick, nervous Irishman will stay in Ajax Bay as a surgeon, along with Lt Col Jim Anderson, a bluff and hearty Scot who's his anaesthetist. He and Bill McGregor greet each other like the old friends that they are. The others will eventually move forward to Fitzroy again, to re-establish the Forward Dressing Staion there. The majority are badly shaken by the unpleasant events on *Sir Galahad* and we can well understand their

* Like the fuselage fragment of p. 16, also now in the Fleet Air Arm Museum.

reaction. One or two get very aggressive and even imply their reluctance to continue soldiering. They benefit from a quiet talking to, and a little walk around the back. The bomb in the 'fridge', now surrounded by white tape barriers, is still easily visible. We know how they feel because we've been along the same emotional route ourselves. Thankfully, equilibrium is restored, and our new visitors will surely end the war on a high note.

Thursday, June 10

A sad day in the history of the Red and Green Life Machine. For all sorts of very good reasons we are to be broken up. With Charles Batty and his support up in Teal Inlet, it's now been decided that Bill McGregor and his team must move forward to Fitzroy. By operating there in conjunction with Major David Jackson's surgical group, he'll provide the right blend of skill and experience close to the front line. Jim Ryan is staying back with us, and we've also been joined by another Naval team, Surgeon Lieutenant Commander Tony Mugridge and Surgeon Lieutenant Sean Tighe, his anaesthetist. They were somewhere up in the Persian Gulf when the Falklands caper started. Having fixed the wounded from the retaking of South Georgia, they've now ended up here in Ajax Bay. After nearly twenty moves between a dozen ships, they're pleased to be somewhere that they can call 'home', even if it's only for a week.

Some tremendous news from the CO. He's asked for help in obtaining more water heaters from American sources of supply. I'm not sure how he's made the contact, but suspect that his being landlord of Ajax Bay has meant some form of rental payment in the shape of a few minutes' chat to London on the Satcom! The African Queen is certainly dying in glory; she must keep going until her dozen daughters arrive.

Another brief on *Fearless* with the Divisional Staff, including Surgeon Captain Blackstone, enables me to tie down the final attack details. Back in Ajax Bay we're still ferrying customers to *Uganda*, so I hitch-hike a ride out and keep her command structure in the picture about the planned assault.

There is a sad little ceremony before we return less than twenty minutes later. Paul Callan, the young 45 Commando chef, so grievously injured on the night of May 27 when we were bombed in Ajax Bay, has finally died of his wounds. Following up, the tremendous efforts of Bill McGregor and

130

Malcolm Jowitt, Roger Leicester has done his very, very best but despite three operations and over 30 pints of blood, the young marine's exhausted and badly injured body has given up the ghost.

Slow marching, a detachment of *Uganda*'s bandsmen ascend the ramp. The body bag is loaded into the cabin, the flight deck party snap off a sad salute that shows on their faces, and we lift off again to deliver Paul Callan to Ajax Bay once more, for burial with his mates.

Friday, June 11

Tonight's the night for the final assault, but today's the day that the Red and Green Life Machine goes Green – and Brown. All the remaining red-bereted elements move forward to Fitzroy this morning and we're sad to see them go. There's still much to do, but somehow we all have the feeling that an important episode in our lives is drawing to a close.

If I'm sad, there are plenty of distractions as we try to distribute equipment and personnel loads evenly between the various types of helicopters which turn up. There is also some mail – April's Mess Bill from the Royal Marines Barracks at Stonehouse in Plymouth! Another rather tatty brown paper parcel, kindly mended by the GPO, contains soap, toothbrushes and toothpaste 'with love from the Wives Club of HMS *Drake*, Plymouth'. How kind those good ladies are, how stunning their generosity – but how have they heard of us?

Early turn-in tonight for all of us. H Hour is at 0200 so we're bound to be in business at dawn.

Saturday, June 12

45 Commando and 3 Para have gone in against their objectives, Two Sisters and Mount Longdon. They're on time and doing well. As predicted last night, first light brings Sea Kings and Wessex in profusion to our door. Teal Inlet is full and Fitzroy very busy. We are getting the overflow, mainly those selected as being fit for travel for 20 or 30 minutes longer. Freed of their human loads, the helicopters soar upwards from the boggy LS, move across to the concrete hardstanding behind the main building, and hook up to yet more pallets of netted artillery ammunition. Their blades bite the air fiercely as they take the strain once again and struggle into the sky with their vital loads. This is logistics for real – broken bodies back and combat supplies forward, with scarcely a breath in between.

The three operating tables are soon in full flow, with Phil Shouler now acting the part of surgical ringmaster. What a change there's been in him since three weeks ago! Like Nick Morgan, his confidence and judgement have come on in leaps and bounds. At this moment there can't be many other senior registrars in the western world with such practical experience of battle surgery.

A Royal Marine chum arrives, injured. Lieutenant Chris Whiteley is the son of Jersey's Governor General, himself a former Commandant General of the Royal Marines. The shrapnel wounds of both thighs and one hand are nasty but not life-threatening at this stage, so it's nice for Major General Jeremy Moore to have someone familiar to talk to when he visits shortly afterwards.

I recognize another of the casualties as a fellow-traveller from *Canberra*. Corporal Jerry Phillips is a compact, muscular sniper from 3 Para. He played the 'man-dressed-as-tree' act for journalists on the way down, and then went ashore to prove his skills in no uncertain terms. Now he's been

133

exceptionally lucky to have taken a high-velocity bullet in his left arm instead of his heart. We debride the wound carefully in anticipation of his eventual return to duty.

Our second Argentinian to die in Ajax Bay then slips out of reach. A nasty, sucking chest wound is deftly sorted out but the patient suddenly collapses as he comes round. Resuscitation is to no avail. The bullet probably damaged the main vessels of the lung, which then tore open as his blood pressure came up to normal again.

Around 2200 the line of customers in pre-op has dwindled to one, an Argentinian lieutenant with multiple shrapnel wounds. He gets fixed up, and business closes for the day. 32 major operations, and our track record for British forces is still intact. At Teal Inlet, Charles Batty hasn't stopped in an all-day session of some 16 surgical operations. Fitzroy has been a bit quieter with eight, but their turn will come tomorrow when 5 Infantry Brigade go for the southern objectives. 3 Para's losses have been heavy, apparently because they had the toughest opposition on offer, Argentine Marines. 45 Commando have lost four men, 42 Commando one. We hear on the grapevine that 42's attack has been a military classic, with the leading company going right behind the enemy in its approach march before joining battle.

So, careful patrolling to identify the minefields has paid dividends in low casualties, but overall the losses are surprisingly small when considering normal offensive doctrine. Attacking units according to the textbooks should have a numerical superiority of three to one, *not* the other way around. And assaulting well dug in units uphill, on foot . . . Hooray for the Red and Green *Mean* Machine!

We hear on the World Service News that today, on Horseguards Parade, Her Majesty the Queen celebrated her official birthday at the Trooping of the Colour. 8,000 miles away her naval subjects celebrate too, in a different way, but with just as much pride and enthusiasm. The boys have earned an arduous duty tot anyway, so there's a bit of finger trouble as Fred Cook and I pour out. Since he would normally have been at Horse Guards Parade, we invite Major Bremner of the First Battalion Welsh Guards to celebrate his Colonel-in-Chief's birthday too. Our new friend is somewhat confused by the toast:

'Gentlemen. The Lord High Admiral –
Her Majesty the Queen!'

Sunday, June 13

Terry Moran's wicked sense of humour has been at it again. The area around Port Stanley is marked on our large-scale wall map with cross-hatching and the bold letters 'SSZ'. We've heard of Total Exclusion Zones and Surgical Support Teams, but what exactly is the SSZ? Visitors who ask this question are given explanations with an earnest and straightforward enthusiasm that implies official truth: 'Spick, Splattering Zone, sir – bring as much artillery down on their pointed heads as possible.'

The visiting personages wander away, probably muttering about our sanity but still not *quite* sure whether the crazy jargon of war hasn't come up with another winner. Who can fail to admire the sense of humour of the official who coined the acronym to describe merchant ships like *Canberra* and *Elk* – Shipping Taken Up From Trade! His perfectly correct answer to an enquiry about further merchant shipping assets would be, simply, 'Get STUFT!'

The southern assault on Tumbledown and Mount William is delayed 24 hours while 5 Brigade get their act together and 2 Para move forward to push through 3 Para's position and go for Wireless Ridge. It's a relatively quiet day for casualties, therefore, while we move our customers back to *Uganda*, but made much more interesting by two very welcome visitors. For the first time since the war started, Surgeon Captain Andrew Rintoul and Commander Andy Gough of *Uganda* are able to come ashore and see for themselves what their hospital ship is supporting.

Now they understand why their patients arrive dirty and naked but looking reasonably healthy. The cramped conditions, field latrines, dust and dirt, and shortage of water are all baseline features of a system in which we struggle to provide life – and limb-saving medical care. A thousand words of description have really meant nothing until today, when half an hour reveals all. I bring them up to date on the battle picture before they fly back on board with the last load. *Uganda* will be out tonight then back in before dawn. She may even have to take patients straight from the battlefields if all three ground medical units gets crowded. They have been clearing decks all day in anticipation, transferring lightly wounded and recovering patients into the ambulance ships for delivery to Montevideo. Apparently, that aspect of the casualty evacuation chain has worked extremely well.

An Air Raid warning mars the later afternoon – twelve aircraft in three waves. They may also have been the ones which attacked Brigade Headquarters up near Estancia House. Again, some of the bombs that dropped didn't go off, and those that did had the effect weakened by thick wet peat. One man was injured but nobody killed. The Almighty must have a green beret.

There's something very different to celebrate tonight. Some unbelievable news has come through about the preliminary rounds of the World Cup in Spain.

Argentina nil, Belgium – *one*! Our morale is as high as it can be when we turn in, early again. It's the Scots Guards', Gurkhas' and 2 Para's turn (again) in the morning.

Monday, June 14

There is half an hour between dawn and the arrival of the first casualties, mainly Scots Guards from Tumbledown. Fitzroy are saturated, and Teal Inlet busy with 3 Para casualties from an all-night stonking of Mount Longdon by enemy artillery. In between helicopter loads of bandaged bodies, the picture emerges of 2 Para fighting through Wireless Ridge with two killed and twelve wounded; 2 Scots Guards completing the seizure of Tumbledown with some desperate hand-to-hand fighting and the cold steel of unsheathed bayonets; and Johnny Gurkha knocking off Mount William without loss to himself, although there are many injured.

Then comes the All Stations and electrifying order: 'Weapons are not to be fired except in self-defence' followed by a situation report – white flags are in profusion around Stanley! There is much to be cheerful about, but a big meat bill to pay still, so operating continues.

Uganda is now taking some casualties direct from the front line, but, as lynchpin to the war's medical effort, I feel that they should be among the first to know of the war's likely end. I jump on a Wessex and fly out to her. The BBC World Service have not yet released the news and so the ship has not received the glad tidings. We have a hurried conference in the Master's cabin and Captain Clark orders two bottles of chilled champagne uncorked immediately. He then pipes for all crew and embarked officers to assemble in the ship's cinema, where I repeat the information to a sea of relieved and smiling faces. With three cheers for Her Majesty the Queen, it's then back to the consequences of war.

The moment that we lift from *Uganda*'s deck and run towards East Falkland once again is now engraved for ever in my mind. The champagne's effect on an empty stomach simply accentuates the colours and detail of the scene. *Uganda* steams along quietly, her white upperworks glowing

138

in the afternoon sun. Behind her, Fanning Head stands out blue and clear in the distance, mute witness to much bravery as well as the savagery and destruction of three weeks' fighting. As the Wessex picks up speed and climbs away from the liner, there's another memorable moment. A steward had pressed a paper bag into my hand as I went up the ramp to the flight deck. In the bag, and now consumed with greater enthusiasm than any gourmet dining for free at the Savoy Grill – a fried egg and bacon roll! No ambrosia was ever sweeter.

We clear most of the casualties to *Uganda* by nightfall and then take stock. Over 50 admissions and 32 operations, the same figure as Saturday. General Moore's victory signal is received and read out as the men stand ready, their tot glasses charged. Tonight the toast is – Great Britain.

Tuesday, June 15

A terribly cold night makes the task of examining the dead more difficult, with limbs set and frozen into unusual postures where rigor mortis has then held them. This has contributed to the unfortunate rumour that two of the dead Scots Guards were captured and then executed by a retreating enemy. The bodies were apparently found with 'hands tied' and 'blindfolded'. Careful examination of the wounds show this suggestion to be nonsense. One has been killed by a long-range sniper shot to the head, the other by a fragmenting mortar round. In other words, they both died on the field of battle. I describe the findings to Lt Col Mike Scott, their charming CO, when he comes to Ajax Bay for their funeral. No more is heard of this unfounded allegation.

40 Commando cross to West Falkland, and Lt Col Malcolm Hunt takes the Argentine garrison's surrender in Port Howard. They discover three dozen or so enemy casualties over there, some with wounds that are a week old and untreated. More work for the surgeons, as we suspected, after the war has ended.

Some of the Argentinians' stories are heartbreaking. Most are starving, indeed some have actually injured themselves deliberately in order to gain medical treatment and hospital food. Others have been shot by their officers, so they say, in the feet to prevent them running away. Once again our surgical policy, based on the time-honoured principles of battle surgery, is shown to be correct. These men have filthy, smelly wounds a week after non-treatment or early closure. The wounds of similar vintage on *Uganda* are not only more severe – they're also much cleaner and healthy-looking too.

It's also Honours and Awards time. Ivar Hellberg asks me to nominate the men of Ajax Bay's medical organisation who are worthy of recognition. The task of picking out those who have risen head and shoulders above the rest is an appallingly difficult one, and I agonize over it. The choice must then be reinforced by a citation, a written justification for the selection which will be scrutinized by the CO, then Brigade, HQ LFFI, CINCFLEET and finally, presumably, the Ministry of Defence.

I put seven names for various awards and all are accepted, endorsed and passed on by the CO. When I finish the final drafts of the citations, one of the marines who has been watching me beavering away comes up, and suggests that everyone in Ajax Bay has got the 'MBE'. My polite agreement that everyone in Ajax Bay *deserves* the MBE but there won't be that many to dish out is met with the protestation:

'No, sir, not the *medal* – I mean the MBE.'

'MBE?' is my baffled reply.

'Yes, sir – Mind Boggling Experience!'

June 16 – 19

Port Stanley is an appalling mess. The logistics advance party sailed around in *Fearless*, then disembarked ashore by helicopter and landed on the racecourse.

The town and approach roads are ankle deep in mud and faeces. There is no sign of any attempt by the Argentine soldiery to build field latrines, or even concentrate their excretory arrangements in one area. Step off the road or recognized path, lift any bush or branch, and some *campesino* has left his calling card. It's no wonder that hygiene is a tremendous problem for the British troops now billeted in the houses. The water purification plant, antiquated anyway, has also been destroyed or damaged by shelling. An aggressive form of diarrhoea and vomiting (known, inevitably, as Galtieri's Gallop) is beginning to take its toll of their fitness.

The Community Centre has been the location of the main Argentinian Field Hospital, seemingly under Air Force control. All their kit has now been centralized in one large room where Malcolm Hazell's men from Teal are now also established. There's no need for them to provide emergency medical cover since Charles Batty and his team are now reinforcing the civilian medical authorities in the town's hospital.

The Argentinian equipment is a curious mixture of the old-fashioned and the thoroughly modern. A couple of the operating tables would look right in a gaslight-and-gaiters Victorian hospital melodrama, but the dozens of boxes of sterile theatre drapes and towels are both expensive and of high quality. Most of the serious drugs are useless to us, mainly because their pharmacological standards differ from the British. The chef and I smash hundreds and hundreds of morphine hydrochloride ampoules for this reason, as well as to prevent their possible abuse.

I'm slightly more cynical about some of the antibiotics.

142

Many of these boxes are labelled with patriotic messages of how their contents are being 'donated for the nation' by the drug company involved, some of them big names on the European market. Mostly these boxes contain brightly packaged salesman's samples, useless to a military surgeon, but no loss to a company loudly professing patriotism and, in truth ignoring it. One box that I open measures about a cubic foot in volume. Divested of plastic packaging, cardboard and other rubbish, the 200 tetracycline tablets that it contains would just about fill a paper cup. The departing Argentine surgeons have also left a message on a board nearby: 'Enjoy your life'.

From the Community Centre the road leads down past the War Memorial and along the sea wall in front of Government House. Sitting forlornly beside one bed, covered in a camouflage net, is a Puma helicopter. The cannon shell holes in its tail pylon indicate Sea Harrier trouble and an emergency landing. Some ground-based hero has also fired smaller calibre bullets into the windscreen, filling cockpit and cabin with glass splinters to add to the other rubbish.

Farther along towards the town are a number of large freight containers, apparently looted. There is food in quantity, thousands of ration boxes spilling out of the twisted doors. The paratrooper on guard to prevent further stealing recognizes me from *Canberra*. My request to try an Argy officer's ration pack is granted, and an intact example selected for me. The variety of its content is astounding, all the way from superb pressed beef through to a miniature of appalling whisky and a charmingly tinted holy picture of 'Our Lady of the Malvinas'.

In the hospital another group of Falkland ladies is busy in a far more practical way. The matron and nurses continue to be splendidly unaffected by their temporary Argentine overlords. The medical superintendent, Daniel Haines and his wife Hilary are both doctors, and also back at work. They were shipped out to East Falkland with their children soon after the invasion, leaving two female medical officers to cope with all the remaining population's sickness problems. Dr Mary Elphinstone was there by accident as a summer visitor; Dr Alison Bleaney is a pretty and tough Scots mum who, as well as suckling her child, was instrumental in persuading the local Argentine Commanders that the British were serious about negotiating an honourable surrender.

With goodwill, renewed water supplies, hard work and the loan of Charles Batty and Dick Knight's skills in the operating theatre, the hospital is soon fully functional once more.

Uganda is now in the outer harbour as well, even more capable than Stanley's relatively diminutive facilities. Men are continuing to step on mines, so the need for surgery persists, sadly, long after hostilities have ceased. With Workshops, Ordnance and Transport Squadrons of the Commando Logistics Regiment also fully established in nearby buildings, there seems to be very little left for Medical Squadron to do. The Army have also sent a field hospital from England to take over garrison medical duties in the long term.

An overwhelming, aching tiredness consumes me. Everything is an effort, decisions are difficult and tempers frayed. I journey back to Ajax Bay to collect my equipment and the rest of the men. There is little space for us in Stanley but Colonel Ivar wants his regiment all there together. I'm in time to attend the last, funeral, rites of our African Queen. A welded joint in the fuel supply has finally parted, and her long and valuable career ends in one corner of a Falkland scrapheap. I also find that my sleeping bag and certain other personal items have become attached to someone else's sticky fingers. Maybe he needs them more than I do, but it is all a sad and slightly bitter note on which to end my time at Ajax Bay.

The men gather up the remaining kit and pack it into the chacons, and then sit quietly in the main building, now stripped of its blanket partitions, stretcher trestles and wooden tables. The air is thick with dust raised by scuffing feet, a ghostly halo visible through the gloom surrounding the three remaining light bulbs. As they wait for the call forward to the landing craft and a brief trip out to *Elk*, on whose steel cargo deck we will sleep tonight during the ride round to Stanley, I walk down through the main building.

Stars shine through the ruined roof of the slaughterhouse, the damp and chill quiet a tremendous contrast to the explosions and searing flame of three weeks ago. The greenish metal cylinder embedded in the refrigeration machinery still looks threatening and evil in the dim light of my torch beam. I resist the impulse to make a hole in the barriers of white mine tape. There is no need to touch the thing once again. We're going. It will all soon be part of a jumble of busy memories. I walk out of the building, and around the side, my breath misting in the cold air.

It was all a happy accident that both taxpayer and investor were parted from their money those 30 years ago. Without their speculation, our efforts for the wounded would have been much less effective. My thoughts are interrupted.

A runner comes up from the Beach Unit to summon us to the waiting LCU. We don our fighting orders, shoulder the bergans and weapons once again, and begin to retrace our steps down to the shore.

The Red and Green Life Machine is closed for ever and, somehow, I cannot bring myself to look back.

The journey round to Port Stanley sets a new low standard in discomfort for the majority. *Elk*'s steel cargo deck, with its minimal headroom and a total absence of heating, is in many ways worse than Ajax Bay. Thoughts about torpedoes cross a few minds but quickly vanish. There would simply be no way up and out in time.

Misfortune deals me a decent card for once. My absent sleeping bag means relative luxury as Captain John Morton invites me to doss down in the chartroom annexe instead. In return, the splendid P&O freighter is donated a small piece of bent Pucara for her cosy Wardroom.

Accommodation is a monster problem in Port Stanley when we finally get ashore. Most households seem to have a dozen soldiers billeted with them, and some have more. Somehow the boys of Medical Squadron and attached sub-units are shoehorned in, and then, like everyone else, the lads take a stroll around the town they've come so far to free. Cable and Wireless are besieged with telegram requests.

The Army have sent No 2 Field Hospital RAMC down to take over garrison medical duties, and there is little left for us to do except repack stores and wait for *Canberra*. The liner has left for Puerto Madryn on mainland Argentina, carrying over 4,000 prisoners for repatriation.

We see our first Hercules too, running in low over the high ground south of the town. Its bulbous snout has been changed in outline by the addition of a long refuelling probe above the cockpit. This particular 'Fat Albert' makes six circuits under a low grey cloudbase before departing for Ascension. Port Stanley's runway is not 'safe' apparently, although the Argentinian Hercules were using the strip right up until the last day of the war. Each circuit is marked by the blossoming of a number of parachutes beneath the open tailgate door. Probably urgent spare bits and pieces for the

Rapier missile units. With some surprise we discover that part of the drop is for us! The American and British supply systems have jointly come up trumps in answer to our problem, and 16 Heaters, Water Portable Immersion, Field Pattern, are delivered beneath nylon canopies. Another four descendants of the African Queen end up, like their ancestor, as scrap when one of the cargo parachutes fails to open. We teach our successors how to use them, and spirit half a dozen away with us. Our field dressing stations inside the Arctic Circle will now be much more comfortable places thanks to these gifts from Heaven.

The Great White Whale welcomes us back on board in the best style and traditions of the Peninsula and Orient. A friendly crew, large amounts of cold beer and up to 12 hours of sleep a day restore the mental equilibrium of a full load of very tired men.

Having promised the Senior Rates in Ajax Bay that my beard would be removed the moment we upped anchor and headed north, I find from the compass repeater in the Crow's Nest Bar that I've been spoofed. We are heading due east! Apparently the Argentinian Air Force have taken to rolling things that go bang out of a Hercules tailgate. *Canberra* therefore does not turn north until we have travelled the best part of 1,000 miles, well out of Harry the Argy Herc's range.

The paperwork begins. As the men relax and clean their weapons and equipment, the staff officers and commanders begin the exacting business of assembling reports and returns. Perhaps the biggest pressure is on John Chester, the Brigade Major. The whole military world wants to know about the detailed conduct of the campaign, the lessons learned, the mistakes to be avoided next time, what kit worked well and which bits were failures.

Life settles into an easy and pleasant routine which would, depending on the cabin occupied, have cost up to £100 a day under more normal circumstances. Outside the temperature rises, the sea takes on a welcome shade of blue, and the sun turns up like clockwork to bronze the lean gods on the upper deck.

For Malcolm Hazell's Troop, *Canberra* is an eye-opening sequence of luxury features after their penance on the LSLs. For them, only four to a cabin is like occupying a penthouse suite. The system that issues replacement personal kit to survivors also catches up with them. With all their baggage about to become part of the official War Grave that used to be

Sir Galahad, none of them have any PT rig or soft shoes. Their new white Service-issue plimsolls are soon modified with coloured pens and added extras. Marine Dave Gowland wins the Troop competition, the first prize a box of beer donated by me, with some rather fancy footwear that Icarus might have saved himself with. Corporal John Clare's humour is visible too. Along the outside edge of his 'training shoes' are some go-faster stripes and the blocked-in words NIKE LEGGIT!

Ascension Island eventually appears on the horizon again, but we do not anchor. Our fortnight here seems a year or two ago, not seven short weeks. There is mail to bring on board as well as a team of Army and civilian experts on clothing, equipment and weapons. Someone in the Ministry of Defence has got it right. The captive audience in *Canberra* has much to say, and quite a lot of it is complimentary. No doubt some of the stronger recommendations of foot-sore infantry will later be downgraded as irrelevant to the plains of Northern Germany, but there is a tremendous fund of new knowledge to tap into.

We steam on, past the Equator, and the debriefings continue. The BBC World Service is piped into every cabin, along with an endless flow of heavy-metal rock music provided by enthusiastic Royal Marine disc jockeys. I give up counting how often *Bat out of Hell* tries to warp the deckhead speaker fitting. Trouble flares in the Lebanon. A rumour spreads around the ship that we will turn right into the Mediterranean, draw some more ammunition and then go into Lebanon to sort out the PLO! No one seems particularly worried by the prospect. Next day, the buzz changes. Royal Marines have Gibraltar on their beret badges, so now we're going to Land in Algeciras Bay, annex the Costa Plenty and only hand it back in return for the uninterrupted future of the Rock!

But the Straits of Gibraltar and Cape Trafalgar are left astern as well, and the Canary Islands appear next. A Spanish civilian helicopter pilot makes half-a-dozen cautious circuits of a strange looking *Canberra* before he allows himself to be waved on to the midships flight deck. He seems unhappy there because, as soon as passengers and luggage are disgorged, our new aviator friend simply lifts and shifts

149

for home. The poor marshaller then gets it in the neck from the Bridge for allowing him to go.

The annual garden party of the Canberra Medical Society is held on another hot midday, and brings its professional and social programme to a splendid close. With a guest list that reflects our feelings for a ship that has done *everything* possible for the medical fraternity in their labours on board, a lot of chilled white wine disappears down relaxed and thirsty throats. The sunlit Captain's deck is a happy scene as I present Peter Mayner, in a short speech, with the Society's Record of Proceedings. Our applause is echoed from the flight deck below, now a mass of bronzing bodies. There is none of the barracking and jeering that one might otherwise expect. Clearly, Royal has decided that his medics are good news and have also earned their fun.

More parties when the Seniors' Mess invite the Officers down the spiral staircase from the Crow's Nest Bar into the Meridian Room. Another Naval tradition at the end of a long passage home is the 'sod's opera'. The entertainment is by the lads and for the lads. There are only two basic rules. First, the Commanding Officer must sit in the front row and take some stick, and secondly, at some stage he must actually take a part in the proceedings. A tidal wave of beer and good humour settles a few old scores painlessly, and also reveals some surprising talents.

The Band are in the thick of things, having earned every bit of their R and R. Captain John Ware, their boss, even produces a piece of music entitled *San Carlos March*. Cleverly interlinking the regimental marches of the various participating units on D-Day, the composition sounds splendid.

The sea grows darker again and the air is cooler. We are turning the corner into the Western Approaches. All the pressure to bring *Canberra* back into Plymouth, home of the 3rd Commando Brigade, has been ignored. For most of us, Devonport would be more convenient and nearer our homes, but this is *Canberra*'s homecoming, and Southampton is *her* port.

For the first time, on July 10, we see England again as the Lizard peninsula looms out of an afternoon sea mist. Helicopters from Culdrose run a shuttle service for the hordes of cameramen and journalists who flood on board, among them our fellow veterans Jeremy Hands and Robert Fox. Jeremy predicts a monster welcome for us in Southampton tomorrow. We're all a bit sceptical about this – the war ended three weeks ago and the British public soon forgets.

We are buzzed by lots of aircraft of varying shapes and speeds, including a large Nimrod maritime reconnaissance aircraft from St Mawgan. As the big four-engined jet turns in and dives towards us, Phil Shouler and I share the Ajax Bay rallying cry that started with WO2 Terry Moran: 'We're *doomed*!' Much laughter now, as there was then. This great and noisy beast, climbing away near-vertically, is definitely one of ours.

We thread our way through the brightly coloured spinnakers of the multihull fleet outbound from Plymouth in the Round Britain Race. Channel 16 is busy as a number of the competitors call up to speak to their now-famous sailing chum, Ewen Southby-Tailyour. The wistful look in Ewen's eyes as he watches them pass out of sight indicates that as far as he's concerned, we've come home from the war a week late.

There is lots happening on Up Channel night. A wonderful Sunset ceremony is performed for us by the Band. The sound of bugles playing the Sunset Call after *Eternal Father* sends shivers down most spines as we stand to attention while the Ensign is lowered.

An incredible meal follows. Denis Rogers, *Canberra*'s chef, retires from P&O service tomorrow so he's allowed to go right over the top. The souvenir menu contrasts our bill of fare with Menu C of the Arctic ration pack. Four weeks ago it was chicken and bacon paste with the dry and tasteless biscuits AB. Tonight, poached trout hollandaise follows Pâté de canard à l'orange. And who would willingly choose mutton granules and dried peas in preference to fillet steak San Carlos? When the Loyal Toast to Her Majesty the Queen is drunk, the P&O officers share our Royal Naval and Royal Marines' privilege of remaining seated.

The later revelries continue long past midnight as the lights of Torbay, Teignmouth and Exmouth pass slowly down the port side. Are those car headlights being flashed at us? It ems possible. *Canberra* is dawdling at half-spead, in order to arrive alongside in Southampton at 1030 tomorrow. It promises to be a long day.

Sunday, July 11

Breakfast is rather early and some of the smarter young subalterns have arranged for champagne at table with which to entertain their company commanders. A festive end-of-term spirit pervades the air, and by the time we're in the Solent a flotilla of cabin cruisers and speedboats has joined us. The P&O ferry *Dragon* slices along off our port quarter, her lines blurred in the tremendous heat haze. The excitement increases as a shiny red Wessex settles smoothly on the flight deck and the Prince of Wales arrives on board.

Later, we meet him at a large reception in the Meridian Room. He seems keen to speak to each and every one of the 400 men and women there to greet him, but time is obviously short. Because we have served together in HMS *Hermes* I'm able to introduce him to quite a number of the men from Ajax Bay. Then modestly, and typically, he flies back to London, anxious not to distract any of the forthcoming welcome by his presence. Only later do we discover that he has also visited every single one of the Falklands wounded still in Service hospitals.

And what a welcome it turns out to be. As *Canberra* enters Southampton Water it seems that most of southern England has emptied for the day. There's a sea of faces on the Hamble side, countless waving banners, tooting car horns, and shouted greetings almost inaudible with the helicopters circling overhead and the liner's own deep bass whistle sounding occasionally in acknowledgement.

Eventually the press of smaller craft around *Canberra*'s salt and rust-stained hull becomes so great that we have to slow to walking pace while the Harbour Police try to restore some semblance of order and safety. There is now time for the Royal Marines who crowd the rails to savour the incredible sight.

Two nubile ladies on a 40-foot gin palace below strip off

their suntops and wave some splendid mammaries in welcome. A section of the onlooking crowd cheers loudly and suggests that further developments should be revealed. The girls seem keen to oblige, but the spoilsport at the wheel stops them.

Eventually our pier comes into sight, again obliterated by signs, placards and upturned faces. Six Army Lynx helicopters drone overhead, trailing red smoke. The repeated singing of *Rule Britannia* is accompanied on certain faces by tears of joy, excitement and pride rolling down tanned cheeks. Up go the balloons, down go the gangways, and then it's back to military life as we've always known it. Hurry up and wait.

Four hours later, with Susie driving, I keep looking at my son and then out of the car window at the passing trees and fields of England. By the time we get to Exeter the sun has disappeared and a steady drizzle sets in. Despite this, every bridge and lay-by is lined with cars and people, ordinary folk out in the rain to greet their returning heroes. The road down into Plymouth itself is almost completely blocked by a crowd of over 20,000. We get through eventually, but only after much hand-shaking and back-slapping.

For almost everyone else in the Task Force, the homecoming will be the same. My house has been decorated with banners and bunting, unknown to Susie. Overwhelmed, I stand outside in the soft Cornish rain as my neighbours leave their houses and walk over, faces wreathed in smiles. More pumping handshakes and silent, fierce embraces. In every case, the message is the same:

'Thank you, thank you *all* for what you've done for us – and welcome home.'

Postscript

Although the *London Gazette* was not officially published until Monday, October 11, a weekend media leak became a trickle, then a sudden flood. On the previous Friday, a number of us were called in to Lt Col Hellberg's office and handed thick white cartridge paper envelopes marked 'Honours in Confidence'. Our families could be told, but no one else. Like Ivar Hellberg, I've been made an Officer of the Order of the British Empire (OBE). It was a huge surprise. I felt then, as I still do, that this award belongs to *all* the staff of the Red and Green Life Machine, not just to me. It had been almost as important an honour to have actually been in charge of the Ajax Bay medical facility, and to have shared every detail of the Falklands experience with this tremendous bunch of men.

When the *Gazette* supplement is actually published, the general excitement over the two Victoria Crosses, although entirely understandable, rather masks the other episodes of heroism described in its quiet, unsensational prose.

All the frigates of that resolute D-Day picket line are there, the Commanding Officers of HMS *Brilliant*, *Broadsword*, *Ardent*, *Argonaut*, *Plymouth* and *Yarmouth* receiving gallantry awards for their leadership during the vicious fight.

From Ajax Bay, Lieutenant Bernie Bruen, Chief Trotter and Flight Lieutenant Alan Swann are decorated for their great courage in coping with the various unexploded bombs on ships and ashore. That arrival of a Scout helicopter outside Ajax Bay on the night of May 28 is also recognized, when Captain John Greenhalgh receives the Distinguished Flying Cross. Richard Nunn is also awarded the DFC, but posthumously. And Robert Fox gets the MBE! Tremendous news.

For Bill McGregor there's a richly deserved OBE. Phil Shouler and Charles Batty are both made MBEs (Members of the Order) as is Terry McCabe for his efforts on the nursing side. Chief Medical Technician Stuart McKinley receives the

British Empire Medal for his devoted management of a vital Ajax Bay feature – the blood bank. A Mention in Despatches goes to Marine Stephen Duggan, so naturally able as a 'medic' despite being completely untrained, that he was sent forward during the final push on Stanley to help the Medical Officers of 42 Commando, Martyn Ward and Ross Adley. Up in the hills and also receiving Mentions for their work under fire in the front line are Leading Medical Assistants Paul Youngman, George Black and Medical Assistant Michael Nicely.

For Captain Steve Hughes RAMC of 2 Para a Mention in Despatches. It's a little disappointing at first, but then a 'Mention' from 2 Para is pretty difficult to get and must be seen in its true perspective. He has done really well, and so have the girls of Port Stanley Hospital, Alison Bleaney receiving the OBE and Mary Elphinstone an MBE.

Some strongly recommended names don't make the final list, which is sad. What's important is that each man (and woman) should feel that they have given of their very best, and that those around them know it.

Uganda's list of suggested honours doesn't get to the post on time, so it's a great disappointment initially when none of her names appear. This is made up for by the New Year's Honours List, 1983. Surgeon Commander Charles Chapman is made OBE, and the Queen Alexandra's Royal Naval Nursing Service also features. The gentle kindness and tough organizing abilities of Sister Jean Kidd are recognized and rewarded with the MBE. A week or so later, her engagement to Ross Adley is announced! At last the fellow's seen sense.

Tuesday, October 12 sees the Victory Parade in the City of London. We'd all like to be there but numbers are limited to an officer and six medical personnel. Erich Bootland and Chief Petty Officer Jethro Young take a carefully selected group up as our representatives. They march, as they always do on Royal Marines occasions, in Naval blue suit beneath the green beret. The Chief of the Defence Staff's eyes widen, as the Corps contingent passes the saluting dais, at this 'unofficial' rig. To the rest of us watching on television, the boys look *very* smart.

On December 14th Rear Admiral Sir John Woodward and

Major General Sir Jeremy Moore are knighted at Buckingham Palace by Her Majesty the Queen. Down in Southampton on that same morning I attend, along with several other medical officers, the inquest on those 64 members of the Task Force whose bodies have been brought back to England for re-burial. Our careful initial examination now pays dividends because the Coroner, Mr Roderick MacKean, listens closely to our testimony and accepts both the evidence of identity and cause of death. In a quiet and dignified voice he pays tribute to their memory by reading out the list of names as a Roll of Honour.

Three months later, Ivar Hellberg realizes those escapist dreams which sustained him through the darkest hours of Ajax Bay. With a 15 man team which includes Terry Knott he succeeds in recreating the famous 'Heroes of Telemark' raid on the Vermork hydro-electric plant in Norway.

And so it goes on. The Red and Green Life Machine has dispersed around the world, with Dick Knight now in Nepal and Jim Ryan in Hong Kong. The boys are in Norway again for the annual winter training and some, like me, have reverted to Naval service. Our paths will definitely cross in the future though. The ships that passed in the night on Longfellow's 'ocean of life' will surely pass again.

There is much to look back on with a quiet pride. The last paragraph of Admiral Sir John Fieldhouse's Despatch of Tuesday, December 14, 1982 sums it all up beautifully:

Major contributory factors to the survival of the wounded were the supreme physical fitness of our troops and the exemplary medical attention given to casualties of both sides. First aid matched the professional expertise of the field and afloat medical teams. Equally vital was the skill of the helicopter pilots in speedily evacuating casualties. Casualties were transferred to the Hospital Ship SS *Uganda*. Once fit for further travel, they were transferred to the three casualty ferries HM Ships *Hydra, Hecla* and *Hecate* and conveyed to Montevideo for onward aeromedical evacuation to the United Kingdom by RAF VC 10. These operations were all conducted with great efficiency and great concern for the comfort of the wounded.

There you are then. The Red and Green Life Machine was merely one link in the tri-Service evacuation chain, and this was its story. For a while at least, John Owen's 16th-century epigram will not be true:

> God and the Doctor we alike adore
> But only in danger, not before;
> The danger o'er both are alike requited,
> God is forgotten, and the Doctor slighted.

Appendix

Names of those who worked in 'The Red and Green Life Machine".

Medical Squadron, Commando Logistic Regt. Royal Marines

Headquarters Troop (21 May – 19 June)

Surgeon Commander Rick Jolly RN
Lieutenant Fred Cook RM
Surgeon Lieutenants Martyn Ward and Graham Briers RN
Fleet Chief MA Bryn Dobbs RN
WO2 Terry Moran RM
Chief Petty Officer MA 'Scouse' Davies
Petty Officer MA Eddie Middleton
Corporals 'Ginge' Worthington and 'Sigs' Rennie
Lance Corporal Billy Noble
Marines Charlie Cork, John Naughton, 'Radar' Shields, Mark Cridland and Pete Pearson

No 1 Troop (21 May – 3 June, then Teal Inlet)

Sub Lieutenant Malcolm Hazell RN
Surgeon Lieutenant Howard Oakley RN
Chief Petty Officer MAs John Smith and 'Nutty' Edwards
Sergeant John Simmonds
Petty Officer MA 'Jacko' Jackson
Leading MAs Jock Winton, Andy Ellis, Rod Cain and Dave Cook
Corporals Tom Robinson, Cy Worral and John Clare
MAs Taff Barlow, Nick Vrettos, 'Porky' Greaves and Derek Whitfield
Marines Fraz Coates, Gene Jago, Scouse Currall, Jock Ewing, Jim Giles, Dave Gowland, John Nelson, Taff
   Price, Ray Whittaker, Robby Robinson, Chris Thornton, 'Tojo' Hughes, Kev Frankland, Taff Evans,
   John Thurlow, Dougy Duggan, Neil Blain and Steve Gosling.

No 3 Troop (from S.S. Canberra 2 June – 19 June)

Lieutenant Erich Bootland RN
Chief Petty Officer MA Jethro Young
Sergeant Paul Demery
Petty Officer MAs Roger Beck and Jack Sibbald
Corporals Andy Christy and 'Pusser' Hill
Leading MAs Terry Andrews and Phil King
Lance Corporals Jan Mills and Jock Inglis
MAs Dave Burdett, Derek Taylor, Mark Penney, Col Glover and Andy Blocke
Marines Mark Bunyan, Jock Cordiner, Gav Fleming, Roy Finbow, Dave Gooding, Col Hewitson, 'Spud'
   Hudd, Gerry O'Donovan, 'Bumble' Hollis, Tim O'Keefe, Dave Needham, Jeff Phillips, Smudge Smith,
   Garry Treacher, 'Timber' Woods and Bungy Williams.

No 2 Royal Naval Surgical Support Team (21 May – 19 June)
                    (from Royal Naval Hospital, Plymouth)

Surgeon Lieutenant Commander Phil Shouler RN
Surgeon Commander George Rudge RN
Surgeon Lieutenant Commanders Andy Yates, Nick Morgan and Tim Riley RN
Fleet Chief Med. Tech. Dave Price RN
Med Techs 1 John Davis, Steve Davies, Trevor Firth, Stu McKinley and Tony Byrne
Med Tech 2 Bob Griffin
Petty Officer MA Chris Lloyd
Leading MAs John Billingham, Phil Evans, Ken Parkin, Dave Poole, Kev Dooley and Alec Pickthall
MAs Geoff Evans, Tom Boyd, Simon Judge, Kevin Shore and Al Wallace
Med Tech 4 Steve Garth

Task Group Surgical Team (7 June – 19 June)

Surgeon Lieutenant Commander Tony Mugridge RN
Surgeon Lieutenant Sean Tighe RN
Med Tech 1 Malcolm Wotton
Leading MA Steve Walsh

Elements of No 1 RN Surgical Support Team (30 May – 19 June)
              (from Royal Navy Hospital, Haslar)

Surgeon Lieutenant Commander Ian Geraghty
Chief Med. Tech. Murray Bowden
Petty Officer MA Bob Johnson
Leading MAs Steve Moutrey and Carl Rich

Parachute Clearing Troop, 16 Field Ambulance RAMC

Headquarters, Reception, Resuscitation and Holding Sections

Major Peter Lansley RAMC
Captain Terry McCabe RAMC
WO2 Brian Apperly RAMC
Staff Sergeant Jed Newton
Sergeants Tich Davies and Chris Fowler
Corporals Stan Wright, Roly Young, Colin Hudson and Neil Parkin
Lance Corporals Sweeney Lea-Cox, Dave Donkin, Mick Jennings and Mac Macleod
Privates Tam Craine, Jock Wilson and 'Fozzy' Foster.
Driver Ally Alich

No 5 Field Surgical Team

Majors Charles Batty and Dick Knight RAMC
Captain Rory Waggon RAMC
WO2 Fritz Sterba RAMC
Staff Sergeant 'Webby' Webster
Corporals Jim Pearson and Gary Seabrook
Lance Corporals Rick Saunders and Roy Haley

No 6 Field Surgical Team

Lieutenant Colonel Bill McGregor RAMC
Major Malcolm Jowitt RAMC
Captain Mike Von Bertele RAMC
WO2 'Phred' Newbound RAMC
Sergeant Russ Russell
Corporals Caddy Cadwell and Colin May
Lance Corporals 'Doc' Holliday and Bob Murdy

Elements 16 Field Ambulance and 2 Field Hospital RAMC
              (from R.F.A. Sir Galahad 9 June – 20 June)

Field Surgical Team No 2

Lieutenant Colonel Jim Anderson RAMC
Major Jim Ryan RAMC
Major John Aitken RAMC
Sergeant Cleverly-Parker
Corporal Wright
Lance Corporals Robson, Lawrence and Elsey

Holding and Treatment Section

Staff Sergeants Stout and Pierce
Sergeant Austin
Lance Corporals Walker, Murdoch and Smith
Privates Ward, Davies, Williams and Henderson

Quartermaster and Stores Section

Major Tom Morris RAMC
Lance Corporals Cameron, Rowe and Bowden
Privates Binnion, Iddon, Menzies, Ward, Jeffries, Thresher, Navin, Pugh, Villiers, Lewis, Brook and Norris
Driver Canavan